THE CONTINUING STRUGGLE

THE CONTINUING STRUGGLE

*Communist China
and the Free World*

RICHARD LOUIS WALKER

 ATHENE
PRESS, INC. ——————————
NEW YORK CITY

CONTENTS

AUTHOR'S NOTE

In January 1957, Chinese Communist Premier Chou En-lai interrupted a tour of South Asia to hurry to Moscow and East European capitals by way of Peiping. The purpose of his journey was to throw the full weight of the Peiping regime behind Moscow's suppression of the Hungarian bid for freedom and to pledge Chinese support for the monolithic unity of the Communist world under the leadership of Moscow. In a joint statement with Khrushchev he stressed that all relations among Communist states are subordinated to the supreme interest of "victory in the common struggle for the triumph of Communism." Chou's itinerary as well as the many communiques issued during his trip dramatized the global nature of the continuing conflict he and other top Communists promised.

Unfortunately the outside world has tended to view developments within the Communist bloc and various crises along its borders in isolation, and has frequently failed to note how internal and external policies are related and how activities on one border are coordinated with those elsewhere. The remarkable correlation of events in connection with the Berlin blockade of 1948-49 and the fall of China to the Communists, for example, hardly evoked comment in the free world.

From May 8 to June 7, 1957, following Mao Tse-tung's call to "Let a hundred flowers bloom, let the diverse schools of thought contend," Peiping leaders allowed almost unlimited criticism of their rule. This period of "blooming and contending" revealed sweeping hatred and opposition especially among the Chinese intellectuals and students, but Mao's organization and control proved more than adequate to crush those who had been brave enough to speak up. The regime boasted of its superior strategy for eliminating "poisonous weeds." Many outside observers had presumed to find in the "blooming and contending" a liberalizing of Communism in China in contrast with Khrushchev's return to Stalinism, only to be proven wrong within a month. Few noted the relationship of the developments in China to the Hungarian uprising—a relationship Mao himself stressed—or to a final bid being made to the Chinese Nationalists for a third united front against "imperialism."

Following Mao's return from Moscow in late 1957, the China mainland press resumed the intense anti-Western line that had been abandoned following the Geneva conference in 1954. By late spring 1958, this campaign reached fever pitch. Because of events in the Middle East and elsewhere, because in most cases the soft line toward the neutrals in Asia continued, and because much of the virulence was reserved for internal consumption, the important turn inside China was hardly noticed. Attacks upon Tito, pressures on Japan, blandishment against Britain in Hong Kong, intensification of rural control, new campaigns against "Rightists" and counterrevolutionaries, and self-confident boasts of new power—these and many other items indicated Peiping leaders had decided they were on the crest of a new wave which would carry them to further victories over a hesitant free world.

This background and correlation with Communist pressures elsewhere were practically ignored when the Communists began shelling Nationalist-held off-shore islands on August 23, 1958. Many statesmen in the free world seemed almost determined not to believe Peiping's assurances that these islands were not the issue at all. It was as though they had put on blinders in order to concentrate attention on Quemoy, thus helping Peiping and Moscow to divide allies and undermine internal support of their governments. Mao Tse-tung and his colleagues have consistently viewed such local battles as part of a world struggle, and they have traded on the inability of the free world to see the overall conflict.

It is necessary, therefore, that we make deep scrutiny into the nature of the Chinese Communist regime, its goals, and its methods. The brief analysis contained in this volume should make abundantly clear the seriousness and the scope of the issues. Nothing, however, matches the eloquence of the Chinese Communist writings for spelling out the total nature of the struggle they wage. I have appended examples of official statements from Peiping and urge the reader to ponder them. Such documents will, I believe, amplify my own analysis and illustrate the extent to which all aspects of Mao's China are subordinated to the great world struggle in which he believes. The appendices should also indicate how far from the mark and how couched in ignorance were the many "solutions" for the Quemoy crisis proclaimed in the press and from political platforms in the West. The combination of the text and the appended documents should demonstrate that we have no choice but to draw the line and burst the Communist bubble of inevitability and infallibility. Until we do, we will continue to move from concession to concession and from defeat to defeat until we have foundered hopelessly beyond the point where freedom can be saved.

The continuing struggle calls for bold and imaginative action by the free world, especially in terms of full economic and moral support for those countries directly threatened by the Communist organizational weapon. But perhaps a prior condition is that we understand the nature of the struggle and the key role of organization in waging it. This is the major concern of the present small volume.

An abridgment of an earlier version of the manuscript appeared as a special issue of *The New Leader* on October 20, 1958. The present text, however, represents a thorough revision and an entirely different focus. Needless to say, I am deeply grateful to the many friends who gave valuable hours to help me with the manuscript. They saved me from many errors. For those that remain I take full responsibility.

Columbia, South Carolina   Richard Louis Walker
November 1958

CHAPTER I

INTRODUCTION

In many respects we have not passed beyond the cliché stage in facing up to the great changes which are crowding upon each other in Asia and transforming its relations with the rest of the world. While many observers, including scholars, repeat pat phrases such as "colonialism is dead," "the Asian revolution," "Asia is on the move," "the center of gravity in world history has shifted back to Asia," very few have progressed much farther. Surprisingly little tough-minded analytical effort has been expended in the attempt to bring the acknowledged great changes into perspective or to project their meaning into the future. For intellectual leaders in the many areas of Asia as well as in Europe and America there seems a distinct preference for the misty nice-sounding generalizations whether based on reality or not.

As regards Asia, such generalizations usually ignore one fact of special prominence. The cultures and institutions there are so disparate and the problems of each country so different that generalizations dealing with the continent are frequently of greater disservice than help in providing understanding of the changes occurring there. For example, there has been frequent neat presentation of a contest between China and India for development as determining the path to be selected by Asia. Such an approach underplays the vast differences between these two countries and their problems, overlooks the degree to which their experiences are really meaningless for other smaller countries, and presumes that these other countries are not attempting or have not worked out their own viable answers to development problems. Assuredly developments in China and India will have influence in adjacent areas, but the impact of Japan—too frequently underplayed by those who stress Chinese-Indian rivalry—may also prove of great significance.

The experiences of many of the inhabitants of Asia during the colonial period; the importation of science, education, and ideas from the West; the problems of economic development; these have provided certain common denominators throughout much of the continent, but the term "Asia" remains preponderantly geographical. It cannot any more be used with accuracy to link such diverse cultures as, for instance, those of Iran and Burma, or economic systems as those of Japan and Malaya, for the purpose of drawing conclusions than can Spain and Russia be lumped together in generalizing about Europe. Even in regions such as Southeast Asia differences among nations in almost every field are great enough to make many generalizations of doubtful value. Understanding the changes taking place in the world's largest and most populous continent must, therefore, of necessity begin with examination of the individual countries.

Another reason for the lack of rigorous analysis of the changes in Asia, where colonial areas have become sovereign states, has been the tendency, both there and in the West, to treat problems within the analytical framework and with the terminology used to describe the unique institutions and history of the West. Thus we find such terms as "feudal" or "nationalistic" being applied to some people and in some areas where nothing exists even faintly resembling what is understood in the West by these terms. Frequently this use of terms and frameworks deriving from experience in the West has aided in creating a basis for accepting the simplistic Marxist interpretation of a uniform progression of history and institutions for all people. The fact of the importation of some Western techniques and institutions cannot justify careless description of the unique cultures and politics of the individual countries of Asia generalized from the development of the West. Such description does disservice to the many newly independent states which are attempting to make their own contributions to the world in terms of distinct national cultures.

Again, many leaders in Asia and in the West urge courses of action with the aim of placating "public opinion" in such countries as India or Egypt or Indonesia. (Some even go to the extreme of talking about or advocating action in terms of "Asian opinion!") [1] This may seem rational in the public opinion-conscious and poll-conscious literate societies, but it does not take into account the extent to which opinion in many areas is not public, but rather the product of organization and direction by a relatively small minority. Many observers who assume that the states of Asia can be understood in the same intellectual framework as the highly-integrated nation-states of the West forget that most of the newly independent governments in Asia sit athwart deep internal cleavages—racial, linguistic, religious, as well as political. In each of these countries social and historical background and internal problems bear an intimate relation to the role they now play and will continue to play in Asia and on the world scene.

Surely this is true of the great new power which has come into being on the Chinese mainland. Like some other nations in the world today—Vietnam, Germany, Korea—China is divided. But the preponderant power, size and population of Communist China and its division by water from the territory of Nationalist China make this a vastly different division.

No change in post-World War II Asia deserves closer scrutiny than the emergence of mainland China under the Communists as a major contender for power on the world scene. No single item in Eastern Asia is more troublesome and complex for the security and policies of the other states there. It encompasses manifold relationships—military, security, economic, ideological—and issues—nationalism, colonialism, racialism. It is bound up in the complex of the relations among the other states in the area and in their relations with the rest of the world. No factor underscores more meaningfully the need to break away from the comfortable drawing-room generalizing about Asia than the organization, power, and militant policies of Communist China. It alone should help to dispel the frequent Western assumption that all people who are different from the West are alike.

The withdrawal of British power from the Far East and the demilitarization of Japan following World War II have left the United States as the only major non-Communist force in the area capable of containing the Communist surge for dominance. It is not surprising, therefore, that Peiping is determined to compel the withdrawal of the United States from the Western Pacific. The United States, committed to preserving the security of Korea, Japan, the Republic of China, the Philippines, and indeed the whole free world in Asia, is in consequence Communist China's chief protagonist in a continuing struggle waged by Peiping. The developments in China since the Communist victory on the mainland indicate that this protracted struggle will not be a simple one. It is important, therefore, that the United States and its allies understand the full extent of the mobilization of Chinese power under the Communists and the manner in which it is employed.

Who would have dared to predict only a decade ago that the leaders of a unified and regimented people on the Chinese mainland would be able to challenge with seeming success in military combat in Korea a combination of nations which included not only the United States but some of the world's most successful colonial powers? Who would have anticipated that in 1958 powerful Chinese leaders would be able to impose such thoroughgoing deprivations upon their people everywhere in China's vast territory that the world would take with real seriousness their claim that they would overtake Britain industrially within a matter of a few years and the United States in a few decades; or that the official organ of the Communist regime would be proclaiming that in comparison with China the United States had already ceased to be a great power? On May 3, 1958, for instance, the Peiping *People's Daily* commented:

> The Chinese people long ago pointed out that the United States is only a paper tiger. Under the present situation when the East wind has prevailed over the West wind, it appears even more ridiculous for the United States to claim itself as a strong power. The United States itself has realized the unfavorable situation it is facing in Asia. In a desperate effort, the United States still pretends that it is strong, like a man who slaps himself to produce swollen cheeks so that he may pass as a fat man.[2]

What is the source of all this self-confidence of the "new China" under Communist rule? Is China really the great power she seems? Is she as powerful as her boasts? Many of the world's great statesmen, including Winston Churchill, and indeed some Chinese, felt that it was a mistake to treat China as a great power when the United Nations was founded during World War II. Were their judgments really as ill-founded as Peiping today would want them to seem? Is it simply a matter of the sleeping giant having "stood up" as the Communists like to phrase it?

Most important, just what is the meaning of the power that is China today? How shall we visualize its policies and position in the world in the coming decade? Will the shift in the balance of forces which it has brought about in Asia and in the world be of the same magnitude as in the past decade? It is obviously impossible to answer such questions with anything approaching precision, yet there are forces operative in China, aspects of the new regime which can provide important keys for projection of future trends. Attempts to assess the meaning of a strong China on the world scene are bound to vary. One American who was not noted for his sympathies toward the National Government of China wrote in 1943:

> A powerful China, militarized under a determined and ambitious military regime and a one-party dictatorship, would not be a hope for peace but a menace more terrible than the militarism of Japan.[3]

On the other hand, in a recent book a Chinese who has no great sympathy for the Communist regime, but who displays obvious national pride in his country's new power, sees a strong China as a balancer between the United States and the Soviet Union and argues:

> The paramount consideration which must be accepted, however, is that a strong China is a force for peace. . . . For only through a strong China can there emerge a healthy power structure in the Far East.[4]

Is the China which has emerged under Communist rule a "menace" or a "force for peace?" And, in turn, what policies will best promote the security of the United States and the free world in dealing with Red China? To answer these questions we must attempt to escape from the clichés and emotionalism which have tended to enshroud discussions of China. The answers depend upon understanding the nature of China's new-found power, particularly its economic base and future prospects. We must be clear and unemotional in relating these to the motivations and convictions of the Communist leadership and the direction and goals toward which they are moving. There are, of course, numerous difficulties in making an assessment of a land where change is so great.

Nevertheless, the following pages should make clear some of the larger issues which will confront China and those who will deal with her Communist leaders in the days that lie ahead. It is hoped that they will also make clear the seriousness of those issues.

CHAPTER II

THE NATURE OF CHINESE COMMUNIST POWER

A combination of the dramatic Soviet achievements in science, especially in the missile field, of Communist diplomatic victories, of the almost unbelievable success of the Reds in regimenting China's hundreds of millions, of developments in the industrialization of China, of propaganda efforts and organization on a world-wide scale, and many other such items in recent years has many in the outside world in a mood to be willing to believe that perhaps Communist totalitarianism can, after all, accomplish the impossible. Many leaders in the West who should know better have become almost uncritically defeatist in their post-sputnik tendency to accept even the most grandiloquent claims advanced by world Communist leaders. Recent revelations as to the extent of Soviet economic assistance to economically underdeveloped areas and the fact that even the Chinese Communists have entered the aid game have given added credibility to other claims advanced by Moscow and Peiping.[5] Communism's dismal failure on the land has been all but forgotten.

Communist leaders hail their advances as proof of the superiority and inevitable triumph of Marxism-Leninism. The special issue of the Peiping *People's Daily* which hailed the fortieth anniversary of the Bolshevik Revolution, November 7, 1957, for example, proclaimed:

8

It is not accidental that the Soviet Union built the world's first atomic power station, launched the world's first intercontinental ballistic missile and the world's first two earth satellites. These are important facts to show that the Soviet Union is speedily catching up with or surpassing the United States in certain vital branches of industry, national defense, science, and technology. They are inevitable consequences of the October Revolution. They are the most vivid evidence of the unchallengeable superiority of socialism over capitalism.

Such statements are usually accompanied with boastful claims of the historic inevitability of Communist victory over the world and declarations that further successes are scientifically predictable. Kuo Mo-jo told the Communist-dominated Afro-Asian Solidarity Conference at Cairo on December 31, 1957, "We are ready to overtake the level of Britain in 15 years, and this is not just a subjective wish." (By mid-1958 "Catch Up With Britain," was the most popular song hit in mainland China according to Peiping.) If we were to judge from such materials pouring from China in vast quantities, the only conclusion to be drawn would be that there are no problems which the Communists cannot solve and that there is nothing but a bright rosy glow of success on the horizon of Red China.

A CAVEAT OR TWO

Therefore, before we turn to some of the very real accomplishments of the Mao regime, a few cautions must be raised. These concern the availability and reliability of facts and figures dealing with the Chinese scene and placing those which are used in proper perspective.

Anyone attempting any kind of analysis of the Chinese economic scene must perforce learn, as the Peiping leaders have themselves learned so well, the fine Soviet art of "Percentagemanship"; that is, how to quote figures without actually giving facts. The rules of this are very simple; there are three:

> 1. Be sure to include at least four figures after the decimal point. This insures that even if your figure has the slightest significance, it will be obscured by the haze of ten-thousandths of one percent.

> 2. Give figures which are a percent of a figure which is already a percent of another percentage figure. This will convince your reader that you are capable of handling the most complex quantities and relationships even if he is not.

> 3. Always accompany your percentage figures with such adjectives as: "great," "victorious," "amazing," "stupendous," "overfulfilled!"

In addition to the fact that Peiping still quotes many percentages for which no base figures are available and that many figures are manufactured out of thin air for propaganda purposes, there are other cautions which must be raised.[6] There are, for example, tens of thousands of collective farms and communes in the Chinese countryside today.[7] Each presumably has an administrative staff to calculate produce, allocate workdays, etc. It is on the basis of their reports that statistical information on agricultural production is arrived at and economic plans are made. Yet the *People's Daily* of July 6, 1956 disclosed that a survey of Kirin province revealed between 30 and 50 per cent of the collectives there kept faulty books or no books at all.

Again, there is the matter of falsification of figures within China by the various cadres and officials. An economist writing for the *Far Eastern Economic Review* of September 12, 1957 pointed out examples of how cadres had puffed up cooperatives and incomes and how economic forces eventually took their revenge and heads fell. The local provincial newspapers in 1958 continued to be full of accounts of falsifications by the "rightists." The article observes that these falsifications are to be found everywhere. For example, a Szechuan cooperative had shown a real 15% increase of income in the year 1955-56; the kanpu [cadres] unblushingly announced an increase of 52%. In Manchuria officials fake the production figures. Elsewhere, 1,700 wells are said to have been dug, whereas there exist only 700 wells. Still elsewhere, official reports purely and simply double the quantity of fertilizer. Or a certain brigade hides 1,000 catties of food, which it regards as its secret reserves.

The important point is that these are not accidents but a general rule, and that the Politburo, the Government and the ministries have only false reports and fake statistics as a basis for drawing up their plans.[8]

The State Statistical Office recently admitted in a self-criticism that there has been no time for penetrating studies of the national economy and that it has been primarily occupied in producing statistics for newspapers and magazines.

An economics professor at a major Peiping university complained during the "blooming and contending" period in the spring of 1957 that it is well-nigh impossible to write on conditions inside China because statistical material even on education, is treated as a state secret. "The joke of the whole matter," he wrote, "is that one can find in foreign books and magazines, especially those from the capitalist countries, information about China which cannot be found here."[9] "Not so!" replied Hsüeh Mu-ch'iao of the State Statistical Office. There are few statistics published "because those collected are not yet fit for publication."

Yet another difficulty in judging China's progress and power stems from the fact that there is little information available giving the breakdown in the various categories of industrial production. For example, with regard to coal production, the figures are limited to gross quantities, and there are no statistics on how much low quality coal and waste is included. The railroad yards at Hsüchow, for instance, found

100-pound boulders in shipments of coal from a mine that had overfilled its quota. At least seven different figures have been released by various governmental agencies for coal production in 1957, a year which despite claims of great increase (more than 10 per cent) in production to 123 million tons (the highest of the seven figures) witnessed a coal shortage crisis and the appointment of a new Minister of Coal Industry on September 26.

These are just a few reasons why any survey of mainland China today must involve a healthy skepticism.[10] There are indications that materials have become more reliable. The figures for industrial production are probably more accurate than those dealing with the agrarian scene. But certainly an air of caution is called for in approaching statistics coming from Communist China, especially when, as at the present time, Soviet weapons advances are likely to reinforce the impression that all claims are real.

One final point must be made. Peiping's propaganda claims and the normal newsworthiness of any observations made in a semi-closed totalitarian country tend to make unduly impressive achievements out of what are normal developments in any growing economy. One economist who visited Red China was particularly interested in the new buildings and housing. "But," he observed, "the new building is not really above the world average; however it is useless to try to convince the New China devotees that the building boom is a world-wide phenomenon, or that incomparably higher rates of development are to be seen in such places as Venezuela or North Borneo."[11] The rate of industrial growth in Japan in 1957 was more than twice that of Communist China, but it was hardly noticed by comparison with the headlines given to Peiping's boasts!

COMMUNIST CHINA'S ASSETS

Having raised the above cautions it must nevertheless

be noted that the Chinese Communists have made notable strides in boosting the power and economic base of their country since they began their rule in October 1949. Some of their gains especially in heavy industry have given substantial backing to Peiping's tough attitude toward the Western powers and the diplomatic and propaganda dealings with the neutralist countries. Mao's claims of industrial progress have in large measure been substantiated by accounts of independent observers within China and by the variety and quantities of Chinese exports to foreign countries of such items as cement, steel plate, power generators, surveying machines, bicycles, and machines for paper production.[12] The following table offers statistics from Peiping showing the rate of industrial growth in five major items achieved during the First Five Year Plan (1953-1957) and the announced goals

	CHINA				
	1943	1952	1957	1958**	1962 (goals)
Steel (mill. tons)	1.2	1.35	5.24	6.25	12.0
Coal (mill. tons)	56.6	63.5	120.00	150.72	230.0
Cement (mill. tons)	2.29	2.86	6.8	7.7	12.5
Petroleum (mill. tons)	.32	.44	1.46	1.55	n.a
Electricity (mill. Kwh)	5.96*	7.26	18.99	22.45	44.0

	JAPAN	BRITAIN	USA
	1956	1956	1956
Steel (mill. tons)	11.11	20.99	104.52
Coal (mill. tons)	46.56	225.57	476.84
Cement (mill. tons)	13.03	12.97	53.25
Petroleum (mill. tons)	.35	.15	353.72
Electricity (mill. Kwh)	73.56	101.18	683.97

* 1941.

** Many of these original goals for 1958 were almost doubled during the campaign for a "great leap forward" that year.

for 1958 and the Second Fve Year Plan (1958-1962). The 1956 figures for United States, United Kingdom and Japan are given for purposes of comparison with current Chinese production claims.[13]

Even granting a certain amount of exaggeration and taking into account the fact that antiquated methods can now be bypassed and the industrialization process speeded up appreciably, the rate of growth of heavy industry in China has been impressive indeed. The July 29, 1957 issue of Peiping's official *Statistical Bulletin* pointed out with obvious satisfaction that whereas it had taken China only five years to jump from 1.35 million tons of steel production to 5.24 million tons, it had taken the United States 12 years to make a similar jump (1.27 to 5.0 from 1880 to 1892), the United Kingdom 23 years (1.29 to 5.03 from 1880 to 1903) and France 26 years (1.32 to 5.30 from 1897 to 1923). By September 1958, the Communists were predicting that steel production, fed by numerous small blast furnaces which were apparently springing up from nowhere over the whole countryside in a matter of one or two months, would exceed 10 million tons that year. But during the third week of October Peiping radio was pointing to difficulties caused by poor quality iron made in the primitive blast furnaces which were producing almost three-quarters of all China's iron, and indicating that perhaps goals had been set too high. The Chinese Communists displayed to the world a few airplanes made in China, claimed that they would produce 40,000 tractors and a like number of motor transport vehicles (a Chinese-made bus began operation in Macao), and in October 1958 were offering knitting machines, road-building equipment, lathes, and chemicals as well as light industrial products for sale on the world market. Although the New China News Agency revealed an emergency directive dealing with food shortages in October, the Chinese leaders had started claims as early as May that the 1958 grain production would exceed that of the previous year by 60 to 90 per cent. Tillman Durdin's dispatch from Hong Kong in *The New York Times* of September 28, 1958 noted, "Foreign students of Communist Chinese developments say many of this year's production figures, in contrast with the relatively reliable final statistics of previous years, are inflated to the point of absurdity." Nevertheless, in general, in 1958 the Peiping regime had at its disposal a remarkably improved basis for building further military power and heavy industry. These remain the major items stressed in the new Five Year Plan.

In addition, the Chinese Communists possess some other assets which must be reckoned with in attempts to assess future prospects for China as a great power. For convenience of listing, we can point to five major assets on which Mao's party counts for further economic development.

1. Totalitarian control

The whole of the Chinese economy is dominated and controlled by the tightly knit and highly disciplined Chinese Communist Party (hereafter CCP). But perhaps no item illustrates more dramatically the effectiveness of the control and the supreme confidence which Mao and his colleagues have in their control mechanism than the creation of the "people's communes" (*jen-min kung-she*) which began on a large scale during the second half of 1958. As *The New York Times* pointed out on October 21, this move appalled even the most dedicated Communists in the East European satellites.[14]

Following the violent "land reform" of 1950-52 which extended party control into the rural villages and prepared the Chinese peasants for protracted class struggle, the cadres began pushing the organization of mutual aid teams and primitive collectives. Then in 1955, with an official urging from Mao, the Communist leadership launched a concerted drive to organize the whole Chinese countryside into agricultural producers' cooperatives, the Chinese version of collective farms. By the end of 1957 Peiping claimed that more than 97 per cent of the farms had been collectivized and that there were almost one million collectives. Control over these collectives proved still insufficient, however, as local loyalties, family ties, and human considerations led to evasion of state regulations and delivery quotas. Following the "blooming and contending" period in the spring of 1957 when Mao's call for open criticism indicated inadequate control even over party cadres and especially among the intellectuals, the regime decided to transfer more than three million people, mainly party cadres, from cities to the countryside, and the State Council issued regulations to prevent their return. The February 24, 1958 issue of the *People's Daily* stated that already 1,300,000 had been sent to the country. These transferred cadres are being used to organize and run the new people's communes.

The move for the creation of communes began with the organization of the "Sputnik People's Commune" in Honan province on April 20, 1958. This commune involved the fusing together of 27 agricultural producers' cooperatives embracing 9,369 households with 43,263 persons. Following Mao's visit in early August to this and other communes organized in Honan, the Central Committee of the CCP passed on August 29 a "Resolution on the Establishment of People's Communes in the Rural Areas."[15] On September 1 the *People's Daily* asserted that the people's commune will be "the basic unit of the coming Communist society." The *People's Daily* editorial of October 1, the ninth anniversary of Mao's regime stated that "Ninety per cent of the peasant households in China had already joined people's communes by the end of September—no more than two months after the mass movement for the establishment of people's communes began." Even though most of these communes were still probably only paper organizations, statements from

Politburo members allowed little doubt thorough regimentation under communes was to be the fate for all China's peasants. The full meaning of such a prospect was very aptly stated in the title of one survey of the commune movement, "The Farmers Become Un-persons."[16]

The essence of the 23,393 communes (about 5,000 families each) which Peiping claimed had been established by mid-October is military discipline and organization of the whole population.[17] It is a determined assault upon the Chinese family, the final center of resistance to totalitarian control. Most communes embrace the area of former townships, though some are of county size. Those in a more advanced stage have already set up barracks for living, "people's mess halls," communal nurseries and tailor shops, etc. Former private residences, which the Peiping authorities began turning into state property in the summer of 1958 are being torn down and the materials used for the construction of the large commune buildings.[18] Officials have expressed determination to take children away from their parents permanently and rear them in commune-run boarding schools. Local papers carry accounts of ancestral graveyards being torn up and the creation of single commune interment pits. Distinterred coffins have been used for building pigsties and in other commune construction projects and gravestones used for roads and buildings. All individual garden plots and individual ownership of smallest items has been abolished.

As the October 1 editorial in the *People's Daily* pointed out, "In the people's communes labor is organized along military lines and things are done the way battle duties are carried out." Labor brigades march off to assigned tasks following a 5 A.M. reveille and roll call. The large brigades, considered "shock forces" and consisting of able men from 18 to 45 years of age and physically strong women from 20 to 25, tackle heavy work projects including industrial and agricultural construction. Men of 16 and 17 and from 46 to

50 and other women from 16 to 45 carry out ordinary field labor as members of small brigades. "Apart from these two shock forces, the old, the weak, the disabled and the children who constitute the partial and auxiliary labor power in the commune are also organized as the 'service team.' They are given various kinds of light labor."[19] Men are allowed two days leave per month, women three days. Minimum necessities are presumably supplied by the communes, but a small amount of pocket money can be earned as a premium for good behavior. The ultimate intention of the communes is to do away with all money as the masses become more conscientious about their joyful transition to Communism. Provisions are made for "work under supervision for reform" of those who are incorrigibly lazy or manifest bourgeois individualism.[20] Needless to say, the whole commune organization is directly controlled by the Communist Party cadres who set work plans and quotas.

Unfortunately, the military organization of the communes is not intended alone for internal control. All able-bodied members under 30 receive military drill every day, and arms are stacked near places of work. The Peiping leaders intend to develop a constantly ready militia force for which each commune will provide a battalion. The full international military significance of the communes was spelled out by Peiping radio on September 2, 1958:

> The broad masses of the peasants, who have gone through the long years of the armed struggle of the people's revolution know perfectly well that military lines are not a thing to be feared. On the contrary, it is only natural to them that the whole population should be citizen soldiers ready to cope with the imperialist aggressors and their lackeys. Although the organization of agricultural labor along military lines at present is for waging battles against nature and not human enemies, it is nonetheless not difficult to transform one kind of struggle

into another. If and when external enemies dare to attack us, the entire armed population will be mobilized to wipe out the enemies resolutely, thoroughly and completely.[21]

It is, of course, far too early to hazard a guess as to how successful will be this Communist attack upon the very roots of traditional Chinese culture and the Chinese family.* But certainly the degree to which the Chinese Communists have already succeeded in pushing their program to establish communes is adequate testimony of their totalitarian control.

Other examples of efficient control over the economy can be cited. At the end of 1957, the regime claimed that almost 99 per cent of industrial production was turned out by state-owned and state-run industries. Even before the launching of the communes the regime had carried through many measures to guarantee that it would procure a predetermined share of production regardless of the needs of the people. For instance, on August 25, 1955, Peiping announced its "Three Fixed" policy: fixed production, fixed purchases, and fixed prices on farm products. Half a billion Chinese peasants have subsequently been in a truly triple fix. Refugees, preponderantly peasants, streaming into Hong Kong have told stories of unbearable deprivations imposed by the state in consequence.[22] In 1957 rationing was extended to many additional items which had formerly been freely sold.

Two other examples attest to the thorough control powers of the regime. Forced labor ("reform through labor service"), according to documentation which refugees from the mainland have presented to the United Nations, plays an important part in the Chinese Communist economy. Some conservative estimates, based on close reading of the Chinese

---

* [For a brief *People's Daily* account of one commune and an official Central Committee statement on Communist plans for the Chinese family see Appendix I.]

mainland press, place the number of forced laborers at well over two million.[23] Another form of coercion is forced migration. In 1956, Peiping claimed to have sent more than 700,000 persons to remote areas for land reclamation. This program was continued through 1957 and 1958.[24]

During 1957 and 1958 provincial newspapers, especially in the western provinces, carried accounts of local revolts, some of rather large size and several months duration, but in every case it was clear that the central authorities had the necessary power to isolate and put down internal resistance.[25] Such revolts could become aggravated as resistance to the communes grows, but to date the tight, capable control exercised over China by Mao Tse-tung has proved a formidable asset.

2. *A unified, smoothly functioning communications and transportation network*

It is difficult for the person not immersed in China and her history to appreciate the extent of disruption during almost continuous warfare in China prior to 1949. In the modern period the internal transport system had never been free from division by foreign invasion and control, marauding bands of dispossessed peasants, warlords, bandit gangs or breakdowns. Now for the first time in more than a century the transport network, though still primitive and poor in many respects, functions smoothly. Further, improvements in automobiles, trucks, buses, and a highway system have aided the transportation and distribution process greatly.[26]

Modern communications—especially the wired-speaker systems—have guaranteed that any decision reached in Peiping is transmitted almost immediately throughout the land. The tight organization and control of the people under the Party cadres insures that such decisions are carried out everywhere and rapidly. Once announced, the Party line on any subject becomes within a matter of hours the subject of discussion meetings and intense study throughout China. The fact that all communications (including the press) and transportation are state-run is, of course, crucial.

3. The vast reservoir of manpower

China's burgeoning population enables the Peiping regime to embark on mass labor projects without having to consider either labor costs or the human equation. The Chinese peasants, inured to hardships and deprivations, are being mobilized for colossal construction projects such as dams, canals, irrigation systems, and road building.[27] One of the most publicized of these great mass labor projects in 1958 was the Ming Tombs reservoir near Peiping where all sorts of high-ranking personages joined "volunteers" for "obligatory labor" in lifting shovels. Even Mao Tse-tung and foreign diplomats joined in the exercise. According to the *People's Daily* of June 10, 1958, more than 317,000 people had participated in the project for their proletarian education in the first four months.[28]

Another example of Mao's ability to ignore labor costs is the drive to increase steel production in 1958. Throughout the countryside effort was concentrated on producing pig iron in 350,000 primitive and hastily constructed blast furnaces. "In each twenty-four-hour period these require the services of fifty to sixty workers in order to turn out a few hundred pounds to a few tons of pig iron."[29]

More will be said below indicating that perhaps China's great population may not be such an asset after all. Mao's ability to draft Chinese masses for military support and enhancement of national power, however, is assuredly a vital factor in his calculations.

4. The Soviet Union

The USSR is both a model and an expected source of help. Peiping pointed out in its adulatory propaganda dealing with the fortieth anniversary celebrations in November 1957 that over half of the steel production—almost 80 per cent of the First Five Year Plan increment—was produced in plants built with Soviet help. Soviet advisors are attached to every Ministry in the Chinese Communist Government and the *Kuang Ming Daily* of January 25, 1957 even referred to a Soviet Advisor-General to the Cabinet.[30].

Chinese pride and nationalism have led to several overt expressions of desire to dispense with these advisors. For instance, the *Kuang Ming Daily* in Peiping referred on June 3, 1957 to the possibility of reducing the number of Russian advisors. But in the midst of the economic difficulties a few months later, the *People's Daily* pointed out on October 23, that the Soviets would play a key role in the projected revival of old factories, and again on October 28, that "Big Brother" advisors were helping with the reduction of overly ambitious plans for the Wuhan industrial complex.

The Chinese Communists count on Soviet assistance and have drawn their new plans with the assumption that it will continue. Figures made available at the end of 1957 set Soviet aid at more than $2.2 billion since Mao's trip to Moscow in 1950. Most of this is in the form of low-interest loans. Soviet assistance has not been as "great and unselfish" (to quote Mao's words) as the Chinese would like; in fact, as a trading partner the Kremlin has proved a rather hard bargainer.

In 1957, 50 per cent of China's foreign trade was with the Soviet Union, and since the early years of the regime more than 75 per cent of China's trade has been with the Communist bloc. By 1958 the Soviet Union was the sole creditor of Communist China. Peiping had run up a debt of more than 5.2 billion yuan (U.S.$1 = 2.4 yuan at official rates). In return for Soviet machinery, petroleum products and ferrous metals the Chinese sent the Soviets foodstuffs (40.4 per cent of Chinese exports to the USSR in 1956), metallic ores (16.5 per cent), silk, tung oil, jute, wool, and other products. For its import of more than one million tons of soya beans in 1956 the Soviets paid the Chinese 380 rubles per metric ton (U.S.$38 at black market rate), appreciably less than the international market price. Yet the Soviets charged the Chinese more than international market price for steel plate. One survey points out that Peiping is paying the USSR at least 30 per cent more for articles than the current price in Communist China.[31] Nevertheless, all indications are that Mao is willing to pay the price for international Communist solidarity and that Peiping is counting on the Soviet Union and other Communist countries for most of the materials to build further China's economic power base.

5. China's new prestige

The Communists have not hesitated to gamble scarce resources in order to win admiration abroad. For example, in 1957, the mainland exported cotton cloth abroad to 28 countries, despite the fact that the inadequate ration at home was cut twice during the course of the year.[32] Again, Peiping was willing to offer limited numbers of such items as cars, buses, and road-building equipment for sale in Southeast Asia in 1958 at prices lower than those being paid for the import of the same items from abroad.

Many of Red China's activities and policies abroad, to be discussed in more detail later, are devoted to building up the impression of increasingly successful and stable prospects for China under Communism. The prestige which has already attached to Mao's China proves an important asset not only in dealing with such countries as Japan and members of the neutralist bloc, but it is of first rank importance in Peiping's relations with Moscow.

A major component of this prestige asset is the very tangible military strength at Peiping's command. As a result of the Korean War and of modernization since, Mao's military forces must be considered formidable. They constitute an asset upon which Peiping capitalizes frequently in policies toward adjacent areas in Asia. The Chinese ability to send more than 2,000 modern jet planes into the air and field more than 2 million troops adds immeasurably to the weight Peiping carries at any conference table, and Mao and his cohorts obviously realize this.

COMMUNIST CHINA'S PROBLEMS

Having emphasized some of Communist China's major assets, it is necessary to point out the very pressing problems which lead to the conclusion that *China has not entered the ranks of the great powers and is unlikely to do so soon!* Most of the Chinese achievements to date can be traced to a combination of Soviet assistance, the utilization of already existing capacity, the ability to control consumption and distribution of foodstuffs, and the expropriation of private resources in China. Present figures, of which we are not too sure anyway, must be projected against the background of China's size, disparity, and resources—and the probability that much of the capital which aided expansion of the economy will not be available again. Here are some of Peiping's major problems:

1. Population

There is a general tendency to view population problems as long-range, and many Western economists who have analyzed the China mainland economy have not bothered to include population problems in their projections. But *China's population problem is pressing and immediate!* It would be difficult to overestimate it. A combination of mass sanitation and health campaigns, internal peace for the first time in a century, modern drugs, and other factors has resulted in a rate of increase which, according to a Shanghai publication "has reached a completely anarchic state."[33] According to one set of official figures in *Economic Research* (Peiping, No. 2,

1958), population increased by more than 76 million during the First Five Year Plan or more than 15 million each year.

Figures for the rate of increase range from 2% to 3% with the most commonly given figure at 2.22%. What this last figure means is that 15 years from now, when Mao plans to overtake Britain in the production of steel and other major industrial commodities, China will have added more than 240 million people, or almost five times the population of Britain, to its already overpopulated land. Or again, this figure means that at the end of 11 years, China will add more people to its present population than there are people in the United States today!

Some of the full implications of the population problem became manifest in 1954, and the following year Peiping began a program for legalizing abortion, encouraging late marriages and introducing birth control on a large scale.[34] By 1957 this program was in full swing. Women's magazines carried diagrams and discussions in full detail dealing with methods of contraception. On October 25, 1957 Peiping's *Kuang Ming Daily* reported great increases in purchases of contraceptives by the people over the previous year and claimed, "Specialists say that the qualities of our contraceptive agents have been improved over last year, some having reached the international standards." It did not reveal what international body set such standards.[35] But by the spring of 1958, it was clear that the Communist campaign to introduce knowledge of birth control had failed; it may have alienated many Chinese by its crudeness.

Peiping returned to its former Marxist position that there is no such thing as overpopulation and roundly condemned as neo-Malthusians and bourgeois "Rightists" some of the very people whom it had allowed to speak up. An article published in the journal *Planned Economy* (No. 6, June 9, 1958) delivered a stinging Marxist rebuttal to a statement on population by Ma Yin-ch'u, head of Peiping University, which had been published by the *People's Daily* a year before. The title of the article which urged more careful study upon Mr. Ma is: "It is Good to Have a Large Population." An editorial in the Shanghai *Wen Hui Pao* of August 14, 1958 condemned those who urged the Party to be concerned about China's population as "bogus scientists who lived on peddling fallacious theories." Said the editorial:

> Agricultural economists of the bourgeois class insist that the backwardness of our country is due to its huge population whose growth outstrips the pace of our production . . . there is one thing of which we are certain. Men are most valuable and the more we have, the better we can accomplish our work. As long as there are men, there will be boundless development of production. It is not because we had too many men nor because of the effect of the "law of diminishing returns of land" that we were poor or our grain production could not be raised quickly. It was because of imperialist aggressions, the reactionary Kuomintang rule and the yoke of the landlord oppression which fettered the development of our productive forces.[36]

The position that a larger population means only greater strength and greater production fitted in with the line of the "big leap forward" and Peiping's 1958 pose before the world as an unchallengeable great power.

Despite the ambitious program of resettlement and reclamation of waste land, official figures showed that cultivated land had been expanded less than 1 per cent per year during the first Plan (107,919,000 hectares in 1952 to 112,660,000 hectares in 1957). Put the other way, on May 5, 1957, the *People's Daily* admitted that between 1953 and 1956 cultivated land (including industrial crops) had declined from .462 to .445 acre per person. The June 6, 1958 issue put the figure for 1958 at .429 acre per person. This includes marginal land as well as land on which industrial crops are cultivated. At the very moment between 4 and 5 million are being added to China's labor force every year, and neither the countryside nor the cities seem able to accommodate these numbers. The most optimistic estimate by a Japanese economist is that Chinese industry might be able to absorb 1.3 million workers per year at its present rate of growth. The Chinese Communists estimate only 800,000!

China's cities and towns are bulging at the seams. Urban housing construction is far below the level required to keep up with the present rate of growth let alone handle the great influx from the collectivized countryside. In brief, this seems to be a key item in the future of China, one the Communists are unlikely to control. The United Nations Economic Commission for Asia and the Far East concluded its survey of 1957 with the observation that "population pressure, as well as the related problem of unemployment and underemployment, is one of the most serious problems facing mainland China."[37]

Of course, the problem of population explosion in the wake of developments in modern medicine and sanitation measures has not been limited to mainland China.[38] The long-run significance for China as opposed to other areas lies in the contrast between Peiping's approach to the resultant food problem and that adopted elsewhere. In Taiwan, for example, major investment emphasis has been placed on agriculture and the development of fertilizer industry, and

	Duration of the Plan	Agriculture and Irrigation	Transport and Communication	Power	Industry and Mining	Social Service	Others
China							
Mainland	1955-1957	8.0	11.7	2.8	40.9	18.6	18.0
Taiwan	1955-1956	47.3	8.7	10.4	27.5	—	—
Ceylon	1954/55-1959/60	36.5	33.1	—	4.4	16.0	10.0
Cambodia	1956/1970	38.0	34.0	4.0	—	19.0	5.0
India	1956/57-1960/61	21.0	29.0	9.0	19.0	20.0	2.0

although the island's population is growing at a rate even faster than that of the mainland (34 per 1,000) it has been able to increase per capita food consumption as well as exports of foodstuffs abroad year by year. The table on page 27 indicates the contrast between Communist and other approaches in Asia to the population and food problem in terms of percentage distribution of planned public expenditures:[39]

2. The peasant problem

Closely related to the pressure of population upon land is the peasant problem. The title of the *People's Daily* editorial of July 1, 1958 indicated that the Chinese Communists understand this: "The Peasant Question Still Remains the Fundamental One." Despite the fact that practically all of China's peasants are being pushed into people's communes where their consumption can be controlled and their activities supervised, despite the dispatch in late 1957 and early 1958 of millions of disgruntled cadres, intellectuals and school children, to the rural villages, and despite such drives as the 1958 year of "a great leap forward" during which Mao told the people they must achieve "greater, faster, better, and more economical results," there is real doubt that even the tightest discipline can force the Chinese peasants to produce more and eat less. A Reuters dispatch from Peiping of December 23, 1957 pointed out an official admission that the few independent peasants were growing 30 per cent more per acre than the agricultural producers' cooperatives (Chinese version of collectives.) Local newspapers report on increasing tendencies (Mao calls them contradictions) toward individualist and capitalist mentalities among the peasantry, of more and more local resistance, of tensions between peasants and urban cadres, and of continued "blind influx" of peasants into the cities. Such developments may even be aggravated by peasant reaction against being driven into the people's communes.

Peiping's approach to the more than half a billion peasants upon whom the grandiose plans for industrialization depend, has been one of supreme confidence. As indicated above the Communist leaders have not hesitated to attack family and cultural values rooted deep in the Chinese country-side, nor have they hesitated to follow the Soviet pattern for industrialization which practically ignores the countryside. This remains true for the Second Five Year Plan, though less so than for the First Plan. The attempt to handle the peasant question through commune control is likely to lead to even greater failure than in the Soviet Union, and in view of the population problem the resultant price can be appalling. Growing peasant apathy and passive resistance can only cause further suffering among the peasants themselves.[40] This could well grow to the point where the very armed battalions the Communists have created in the communes are turned against them.

3. Geography

Although China is one-sixth again larger than the United States, it has less than half as much arable land as the United States. Peiping's figures claim 278,270,200 acres of cultivated land in 1957. This compares with 380 million acres used for crops and 526 million acres used for grassland and pasture in the United States in 1954.[41] China's climate and rainfall are frequently unreliable and the possibility of flood, drought, or other natural disasters is ever present, especially in the marginal agricultural areas into which the Communists have pushed the "volunteer" settlers.[42] Doctrinaire concentration on heavy industry again in the Second Five Year Plan would seem to preclude adequate development of the necessary chemical fertilizer industry which offers the biggest hope for rapid increases in agricultural production. It should be noted, however, that the *People's Daily* of January 21, 1958 promised an output of five to seven million tons in 1962 under the amended draft of the Second Plan compared with a claimed production of more than 700,000 tons in 1957.[43]

China's resources are poor and outside of Manchuria no really good concentration of industrial raw material potential has yet been discovered. The distance of the limited oil discoveries in Kansu and Sinkiang from the centers of population, for instance, confront Communist economic planners with a major transportation problem. Frequent shakeups in the Ministry of Petroleum Industry, such as the removal of Li Chu-kuei as minister on February 12, 1958, have indicated official frustration over inadequate petroleum reserves.[44] In August 1958, the New China News Agency announced discovery of great new oilfields near Nanchung in central Szechuan province. These turned out to be fields already explored and estimated by the Nationalists during World War II. Peiping estimated that these "big reserves of good quality petroleum" would produce only 50,000 to 120,000 tons of crude oil in 1958.[45] Although the Communists predicted glowing success for their 1958 steel production program, by October there were official admissions that it may have been too ambitious. One of the reasons for this was revealed when representatives from twelve provinces suffering serious shortages of coal met at Paofeng, Honan on October 18. The Vice-Minister of Coal Industry, Ho Ping-ching stated at the opening of the conference, "The shortage of coal for iron and steel production has been a very critical problem since last September."[46] Despite frequent boasts of new raw materials discoveries, China does not at present possess the requisite raw materials base for a super-power.[47]

As noted above, the transportation system has been unified and is running smoothly, but it is still grossly inadequate. The railroads handle more than two-thirds of the internal transport tonnage (more than 80 per cent of that moved by modern means), but there were still only 18,053 miles of track in all of China at the beginning of 1958. Even this figure is misleading, because over 40 per cent of this mileage is in Manchuria and many of the new lines have strategic importance but are of little economic value. This compares with 220,500 miles in the United States; it is about equal to the railroad mileage for only the three Middle Atlantic States: New Jersey, New York, and Pennsylvania (18,567 miles). In connection with the 1958 big leap forward Railway Minister Teng Tai-yuan spoke in Peiping on September 28 about a railroad crisis caused by a shortage of railway cars and inadequate facilities. He called for special labor armies to speed the loading and unloading of cars in order to speed the flow of cars.[48]

Highways and other modes of transport are even less adequate. Furthermore, the Chinese people are divided by usually barren and inhospitable mountain terrain and language barriers. Although the Chinese system of writing can surmount most spoken language barriers, less than 15 per cent of the population is sufficiently literate to handle any but the most elementary problems; most of the literates are in the cities. In brief, China's geography does not offer easy prospects for the bright future as a great world power that the Communists so frequently assert.

4. Minority nationalities

Like the Soviets the Chinese Communists have been plagued with passive resistance, localism, and outright revolt among these groups, and Peiping's hold is far from strong in many of the frontier provinces where most of the minority groups live.[49] They frequently assert that the minorities constitute only 6 per cent of the population yet occupy almost 60 per cent of the land area. These figures are grossly misleading and inaccurate. In the first place, by their own admission the Communists were forced to estimate the population of minority areas rather than carry out direct census. Secondly, in many of the autonomous minority areas that have been set up the Chinese far outnumber the minority peoples.[50] This is true, for example, of Inner Mongolia and of the Kwangsi Chuang People Autonomous Area set up on March 5, 1958 replacing former Kwangsi province.[51] Yet these figures do indicate, at least, that the problem is not a small one. Mao Tse-tung quoted them in his February 27, 1957 speech on contradictions among the people. He stated that both "great Han-chauvinism" (the oppression of the minority nationalities by Chinese—usually the Communist cadres) and local nationalism were contradictions to be overcome among the people.[52]

During 1957 and 1958 Peiping became more and more concerned about resistance in the minority areas. Campaigns were launched against the "separatist ideas" among the young intellectuals; "Rightist" leaders were accused of trying to establish independent kingdoms, and many long-time Communist leaders were expelled from the Party. Revolts in Tibet forced Peiping to abandon plans for socialization there until after the Second Five Year Plan.[53] Peiping leaders frankly admitted that "Local nationalism has become in many minority nationalities areas a dangerous tendency worthy of grave attention."[54] One reason for the increasing concern, in addition to the strategic border location of most of the minority areas, is probably the fact that many of these regions contain raw materials deposits which Peiping needs.

Some areas and groups have proved particularly troublesome to the Communist leadership. In addition to Tibet, Sinkiang and Tsinghai have been in a constant state of unrest. In June 1958, five high-ranking Communist cadres in Sinkiang were expelled from the Party and accused of saying that Sinkiang should belong to the Uighur people and even that it should become an independent republic.[55] Similarly the governor of Tsinghai, a Party member for more than thirty years, was expelled from the Party because of his "anti-Party criminal activities," which included the arch crime of "parochial nationalism." While visiting in Kansu he said that the people of Kansu should rule Kansu.[56]

A major problem in Tsinghai and in many of the western areas is the Chinese Moslems, who are treated as a separate nationality. Since the summer of 1957 the Communist leadership has been extremely hostile in its attitude toward these Hui people, or Chinese Moslems.[57] Peiping condemned the teaching of Arabic in Moslem areas and has even adopted measures for forced migration of Chinese Moslems away from coastal provinces.[58] On May 16, 1958, the *People's Daily* accused the Moslems in Honan of trying "to set up an independent kingdom." Despite seemingly persuasive propaganda about religious freedom directed toward Moslem areas in the non-Communist world, mainland China's press gives ample reason to believe the prominent Moslem leader in China who, during the "blooming and contending" period, cried, "The Moslem people in China are in agony."[59]

Mainland newspapers have given increasing attention to the problem of "Rightist" and "bourgeois" tendencies among the minority peoples, and it is difficult to judge whether Peiping's toughening attitude is a cause or a result of growing resistance. In any event, the Communist determination to bring the national minorities under collective control and to exterminate the religions and customs which resist that control is hardly likely to lead to an easy solution of a problem which China shares with many other countries in Asia.[60] It is nonsense to view, as Peiping does, the natural desire for self-government among these people as a "product of capitalism" and "feudal yearning." This is, as *The New York Times* editorialized on January 19, 1958, "part of the typical Communist mode of obscuring fact by repetitious cliché." After discussing Peiping's inflexible and harshly dogmatic position toward the minorities, the editorial concludes, "Peiping is in for trouble, and deserves it."

5. *Commitment to International Communism*

Finally, China's assertion of a key role in the world Communist movement has involved the expenditure of scarce resources for military buildup and propaganda activities abroad—including economic aid to nine countries: Nepal, Cambodia, Ceylon, Egypt, North Vietnam, Albania, Hungary, Yemen, and North Korea.[61] In a country with problems of such scope, where income in some provinces (Szechuan, for example) averages less than U.S.$26 a year a commitment of 18.85 per cent (1957) of the national budget for military buildup can be a source of great misery.[62] The enmity toward the West, an important part of the commitment to the Soviet camp, has resulted in the blockade of strategic materials which continues to hurt Chinese industrial and military plans. In 1957, for example, the Chinese mainland imported 1,150,000 tons of crude oil, a considerable drain on exchange resources. Observers pointed out that at least one major reason, in addition to poor prospecting, was that the Western embargo had prevented oil drilling equipment, also in short supply in the USSR, from getting to China.[63]

Many other major problems could be listed—including modern Chinese nationalism. Chinese may resent continued subordination to the interests of Kremlin-led Communism and their resentment may lead to even more intense expressions of anti-Soviet feeling than erupted during the "blooming and contending" period in May and June 1957. But the five major problems listed above cancel out many of the assets. A realistic appraisal of China's power even at the end of the Second Five Year Plan in 1962 (assuming that targets are met), forces the conclusion that China will still not be a great world power. Rather one must conclude that its agrarian and population conditions make China the biggest problem for the Soviet bloc.

Taro Yamada, Japanese specialist on Soviet affairs, writing in the Japanese magazine *Sekai Shuho* on December 21, 1957, stresses the population increase and states, ". . . only the Soviet Union's self-sacrificing economic aid that can break through the difficulty. But it will be too great a burden for the Soviet Union to support and develop Red China's economy. Support for Red China's economy is likely to become the greatest problem in the Communist bloc."

Yamada believes that the limit of Soviet aid to China has already become the key issue within the Communist bloc. The Chinese Communists are making new requests for Soviet aid at the very moment the Soviets find themselves embarked on a greatly enlarged program of economic assistance elsewhere, when they must now give instead of take in Eastern Europe, and when the Russian people have been promised better standards and more consumers goods. China's size, manpower, and propaganda importance to the Communist bloc give Peiping leaders a great amount of leverage in their negotiations with the Kremlin. As long as Western opposition remains firm, Mao and his colleagues are likely to have to use this leverage to the point where tensions between the partners will increase.[64]

SOURCES OF PRESENT POWER

Given the problems of China at its present underdeveloped state, the task of turning that country into an industrial world power is staggering. Yet the leaders in Peiping exude self-confidence and convey their own conviction that they have already arrived at a power position of first magnitude. We obviously have to turn to factors other than economic or industrial to explain the present power of Communist China. At the risk of oversimplification, I would suggest that there are four key factors on which Peiping leaders base their claim that they have already attained great power status. All four are played up and symbolized in the mammoth parades held at the Gate of Heavenly Peace in Peiping every May 1, August 1, and October 1 before a large assembly of world Communist leaders and visiting dignitaries. Two have already been mentioned as among China's assets for economic development.

1. The alliance with the Soviet Union

Peiping's parades display the most modern types of Soviet military equipment and examples of Soviet aid toward industrialization. Soviet material was the key factor which enabled Chinese mass manpower to be a match for the United Nations coalition in the conventional type warfare fought in Korea and in turn enabled the Chinese to play a key role in turning the tide against the French in Vietnam. It is Soviet equipment which Peiping believes will make possible the "liberation" of Taiwan against the opposition of U.S.-backed Nationalist forces. It is important to remember that despite the persuasiveness of the peace campaigns so frequently conducted by Peiping, there is always in the background a long history of Communist military experience, and frequent displays of military power attest Mao's awareness of its vital role.[65] China's own limitations in terms of industrial raw power are thus to some extent compensated for by the Soviet alliance and resultant military power in being. This is not an insignificant item in Asia where leaders of the many nations that have become independent had to fight for that independence.

Probably Chinese Communist leaders draw some satisfaction from the current trend in Western strategic thinking which accents the build-up of nuclear weapons while at the same time recognizing that the potential for mutual destruction makes nuclear warfare an unlikely choice even at the tactical level. They also know that tactical nuclear arms would be of limited advantage in many of China's sparsely populated, mountainous border areas. Peiping has undoubtedly noted decreasing Western willingness and capabilities for aiding the smaller states of Asia with substantial numbers of infantry prepared to fight attrition-type war, especially in places where the issue is mixed up with colonialism and internal division as in Vietnam and in areas where Mao's guerrilla strategy, discussed below, can be brought into effective operation.

Peiping interpreted United States eagerness to jump at the slightest opportunity for ending the war in Korea as an obvious sign of weakness. Western hesitancy over developments in Vietnam in 1954-55, the manner in which the British and French conducted their operation at Suez in 1956, the consternation within the United States and the pressures exerted on Washington by allies after the Chinese Communists launched their bombardment of Nationalist-held offshore islands on August 23, 1958: such indications of growing reluctance by Western powers to risk heavy casualties short of the great war they will seek to avoid at all costs have undoubtedly contributed to Chinese Communist self-confidence and feelings of strength.[66] Given their mass wave assaults in Korea and the figures on their liquidations at home, it may be doubted whether they are motivated by the same considerations for individual human life as the West.

The enthusiasm with which Mao's regime has carried forth the Soviet campaign against "weapons of mass destruction" (linked, incidentally, with their germ warfare campaign during the Korean War) shows them fully aware that they possess initial advantages in conventional land warfare operations. They remember how China's size and population worked in her favor during the war against Japan. Now there is the additional advantage of Soviet assistance. It is not surprising, therefore, that industrial and transportation planning have been pointed toward maximizing the possibility of con-

tinuous Soviet material assistance in event of future involve-
ments in Korean- or Vietnamese-type hostilities. The USSR
remains the major source for the continued modernization
and building of the "People's Liberation Army" of Communist China.

2. *Organization and Control*

This second key factor behind China's new power is
also admirably illustrated by such parades as that of October
1, 1958 in Peiping in which more than 600,000 civilians participated in addition to the military.[67] In the early weeks of
September that year, the Communists claimed that more than
300 million Chinese had participated in demonstrations
against the United States within a period of two weeks. The
leaders of Communist China, drawing inspiration from the
Leninist-Stalinist model but in many ways improving on it,
have developed probably the most thorough-going system of
political control yet devised. It combines modern psychological techniques and mass communications gadgetry with
Soviet-style criticism-self-criticism and Party centralism along
with old Chinese patterns of mutual responsibility and pressure for conformity. Backed by the ever-present symbols of
force, it grasps men up in innumerable organizations which
encompass every field of activity and subordinates them all to
the rigors of the state.[68]

Peiping's ability to organize and control humans is
evidenced by the mass calisthenics performed every day
throughout China to instructions from ever-present loud-
speakers—even on river boats. The capacity of the regime to
liquidate all opposition of any note and bring a population
the size of China's under thorough control, including collectivization, in such a short period indicates a dimension of
power that dare not be underestimated. The isolated individual who visits China must be impressed by the degree to

which people from all walks of life conform to the pattern laid out by the state, and some of them with seeming enthusiasm. Drabness has been systematized. Foreign visitors are tempted to believe that the force which has unified China under a control so thorough is indeed just what Chou En-lai claims, "invincible." It was following his visit to China, including being present for the October 1 Anniversary parade in Peking in 1956, that Sukarno proclaimed his "guided democracy" for Indonesia. Communist leaders themselves draw confidence and inspiration from the masses bending to commands. Displays of Peiping's organizational power are sufficient to breed a certain amount of defeatism in the strongest opponents of their system.[69]

3. Ideological conviction

The Chinese Communists are determined to follow the path of the Soviets in building their country into a great world industrial power no matter what the cost. There is little reason to doubt their sincerity when they announce their irrevocable commitment to the camp of socialism headed by the USSR. They have followed the line laid down by Moscow through many crises when national interest would seem to have dictated otherwise—the Hitler-Stalin Pact, the Japanese-Soviet Treaty, Yalta, and the Russian looting of Manchuria. In supporting the Soviet moves to crush the Hungarian freedom fighters, in attacking Tito again in 1958, in backing Russian moves in the Middle East, Mao Tse-tung has with faithful consistency insisted on the primacy of Soviet aims and the necessity for Soviet leadership.

We should not underestimate the power of a crusading zeal. The Chinese Communists and some of the youth they lead display a conviction and dedication that has marked the expansion stages of many great movements in world history—Christianity and Islam, for example. Such a dedication is based upon and perpetuates a "we-they" philosophy in which the overriding concern becomes the elimination of the "they." In this case the creed is one which explains China's past history in simple terms and brings it into the framework of world history in such a manner that in the minds of the converts the long-run victory of world Communism is worth any sacrifice. The key element for China is Lenin's theory of imperialism which enables the linking of internal struggles with the two world camps.[70] The ability of the Communist leadership to instill enthusiasm among some Chinese who resented China's recent weakness and division, in the youth, and in nationalists who yearn to restore China's past leadership and prestige in Asia, should not be underestimated.

4. The Asian context

China is a great power in Asia because of the comparative weakness of her neighbors including demilitarized Japan. In terms of modern industrial development Japan is far ahead of China. Yet the importance of the three elements listed above is indicated by the great world concern over China's power and the relative lack of discussion of Japanese power in Asia today. Peiping's impressive parades of its military might, even though termed "forces for peace," have not been wasted on the many visiting leaders from the smaller countries, whose strength is in no way comparable. They realize that they are no match for the Soviet-equipped forces of China. Likewise, in terms of their own aspirations for national power *vis-à-vis* the West, they are duly impressed with the stature that alliance with the Soviet bloc has brought to China.

Although China, predominantly a land power, is still in absolute world terms a weak power when compared with the industrially advanced nations, her relative position in Asia is enhanced because totalitarian control has been able to overcome the internal weaknesses which continue to plague the governments of other states in Asia. This, too, has given

Peiping added power and prestige in the Asian geopolitical context.

There are, of course, many other reasons which can be adduced to account for China's new great-power status. The four factors listed, however, when taken in the effective combination which Peiping has fashioned, certainly constitute a key to understanding how the Communists have been able to overcome some of the limitations imposed by geography, overpopulation, and a recent history of division, warfare, and failure to meet the challenge of the industrial West.

The build-up of China's prestige on the Asian scene is also a matter of a reciprocal relationship. The very extent to which the rulers in Peiping are able to exert influence upon and gain accolades from their smaller neighbors creates a cycle which moves in the direction of according ever greater power and leadership to the new Chinese state. For the newly independent states of Asia there has been a somewhat disenchanting realization that sovereignty has not brought all the blessings they had expected. In many cases the attainment of independence has sharpened problems which existed under colonial control, and the usual goals of industrialization, economic improvement, and equality with the white man are far from realization. In the absence of forcefully presented alternatives the Chinese gain further prestige by parading their totalitarian planning before the eyes of visitors who meet untold obstacles in their less tightly controlled areas at home.[71]

At the Eighth Congress of the Chinese Communist Party, September 1956, Peiping spokesmen, speaking for a world audience and especially an audience of leaders from Asia, stressed their ability at planning and announced that at the end of the Second Five Year Plan in 1962 China would rank fifth or sixth among the world's industrial powers. This presumes a somewhat stagnant industrial development elsewhere in the world and overcoming some of the problems listed above, but what is important is that Communist China is having no small success in posing not only as a leader against Western colonialism but as the leader in Asia of a system which can tackle the planning problems of underdeveloped areas.

CHAPTER III

CONTINUING FORCES

The Chinese Communist leaders have already indicated by their actions that in line with Chinese historical
tradition and Leninist creed they are capable of long-range
planning and strategy which can involve many seemingly con-
tradictory tactical shifts. Expediency in tactical shifts is never
subordinated to consistency. Following the Afro-Asian Conference at Bandung, Indonesia in April 1955, Peiping began
an all-out courting of the neutral countries, talked ceaselessly
of the five principles of peaceful coexistence, insisted on
mutual non-interference in internal affairs, and denounced
military alliances as attempts to divide the world into hostile
camps. Though never abandoned, Mao's 1940 statement that
"In the world from now on, 'neutrality' is only a term for
deceiving people," and abuse such as was heaped upon Nehru
during the "liberation" of Tibet were conveniently played
down. This line toward the neutralists in Asia has continued
at the same time Peiping has changed its line internally and
toward other countries. For example, the June 26, 1958 issue
of the *People's Daily* in continuing the new campaign against
Tito quoted Tito as saying, "We are against division of the
world into camps," and commented:

> How typically the voice of a traitor! How that state-
> ment "against division of the world into camps . . ."
> sounds like the statement "against division of the
> world into classes" written by a deserter from the
> Communist Party who has surrendered himself to

the enemy! Since a number of imperialist countries and a number of socialist countries exist at the same time in the world the existence of camps is inevitable. . . . The socialist camp and the imperialist camp are fundamentally opposite in nature and cannot be mentioned in the same breath.

About a year earlier, following the brief month when a few flowers of freedom bloomed in Mao's garden, the *China Youth Journal* of August 8, 1957 maintained:

There is definitely no such thing as the transcendent Third Independent Course. . . . In the domain of politics and ideology, it is either the easterly wind getting the upper hand of the westerly wind, or vice versa. Peaceful coexistence and mutual non-interference are impossible.

Despite such shifts in tactics, however, there are some forces which will probably remain operative in directing China's newly found power. To a brief discussion of some of these we now turn.

FORCES DIRECTING CHINESE POWER

1. Ideological commitment to the Communist cause led by Moscow

Those who talk wishfully of establishing closer relations with Peiping and attempting to placate China's Communist leaders in order to split them away from Moscow usually overlook the strong ideological ties which have existed between Soviet and Chinese leaders since the beginning of Communism in China.[72] The two-camp view of the world is imbedded in every aspect of the Peiping regime, and attempts at conciliation are viewed only as evidence of weakness in the camp of "the enemy" and further justification for maintaining the solid Communist alliance in order to gain further victories. The Chinese leaders firmly believe, and Mao has stated, that "Liberated China and a liberated world are inseparable," and that "in the present-day world, to reject the Soviet Union is tantamount to rejecting peace." On his second visit to Moscow as head of the Chinese state in November 1957, Mao reiterated his position before the Supreme Soviet:

> Soon after it was founded, the People's Republic of China concluded a treaty of friendship, alliance, and mutual assistance with the Soviet Union. This is a great alliance of the two great socialist countries. We share the same destiny and the same life-spring with the Soviet Union and the entire socialist camp. (Enthusiastic applause) We regard it as the sacred international obligation of all socialist countries to strengthen the solidarity of the socialist countries headed by the Soviet Union. (Applause)

During the Middle East crisis in the summer of 1958, Khrushchev abruptly called off his July 23 agreement for a "summit" meeting following his visit to Peiping July 31 to August 3. A number of observers believed that the reversal had been forced upon him by Peiping, but one European analyst has shown convincingly that the Chinese Communists "parroted the Moscow line on every phase of Khrushchev's maneuvers, including the period when he seemed agreeable to a Security Council special session."[73] Later developments indicated that Khrushchev's visit to Peiping was probably more concerned with joint strategy for the military offensive against Quemoy and Matsu and pressures against Britain and Japan in Asia than with concern over a "summit" meeting. Undoubtedly there is more give and take in Moscow's relations with China than with the East European satellites. But the Chinese Communist leaders have indicated, as Chou En-lai expressed it at the National Day reception in Peiping, September 30, 1958, that they "will spare no effort to consolidate the fraternal solidarity of the socialist camp headed by the great Soviet Union."[74]

Documents in connection with the Second Session of

the Eighth Congress of the CCP from May 5 to May 23, 1958, underscored the importance of the two-camp view of the world and illustrated how this is used to link internal and external events and problems. Internal resistance by "Rightists" and "revisionists" became within the framework of two-camp reasoning *prima facie* evidence of collusion with the camp of the enemy. The enemy is pictured as the camp of capitalism, fascism, imperialism, war, and oppression (plus many colorful adjectives) led by the United States which because of internal contradictions is losing the battle against the camp of socialism, peace, democracy, national emancipation, and liberation (with equally colorful adjectives) led by the Soviet Union.

In the first issue (June 1958) of the new theoretical journal *Red Flag* published by the Central Committee of the CCP, Vice-Minister of Foreign Affairs Chang Wen-t'ien repeated a formula which has characterized pronouncements of the Chinese Communist leadership for more than three decades:

> The basic feature of our age is the existence in the world of two fundamentally opposed social economic systems; with vigorously growing socialism on the one hand, and declining and collapsing imperialism on the other. At present, while the Soviet Union, China and other countries of the socialist camp are making giant leaps forward in production, the United States, at the head of the imperialist camp, is in the throes of a profound economic crisis.

Within this two-camp view, the duty of enmity toward the United States, isolating it from its allies, and destroying its power, becomes an overwhelming necessity. The Party Congress adopted a resolution on May 23, 1958 endorsing the international declaration by the 64 Communist parties meeting in Moscow the preceding November to the effect that the "aggressive imperialist circles of the United States have become the center of world reaction and the most deadly enemy of the peoples."[75] A statement from the same Communist leaders in China almost 25 years before indicates only too well the consistency with which they have followed the two-camp approach. After levelling many charges against the United States, it says:

> All of these facts, in addition to the billions of dollars [*sic!*] which Roosevelt is using for building the American imperialist war machine, show up the "Peace Policy" of the American president as meaningless words. At the same time he is talking about peace, he is building one of the largest and most modern aerial, naval and army forces the world has ever seen. An undeclared war is being carried on through the puppet Chiang Kai-shek. . . . Without American-made rifles, cannons, shells, airplanes, Chiang Kai-shek could not continue this bombing and destruction. Is this what the American president has in mind when he talks about a peace policy?[76]

On reading the almost identically worded charges levelled against President Eisenhower in 1958, the reader of the Chinese Communist press is reminded of a remark by Sir Gladwyn Jebb at the United Nations in 1950. Jebb caused great consternation within the Soviet delegation because of translation difficulties while those who understood English chuckled merrily as he replied to an extensive harangue by the Soviet delegate: "If I might borrow a phrase from the language of American 'bop': Dig that broken record!"

Too frequently commentators on China forget that whether the hate-America and anti-Western campaign is at fever pitch as it was in the fall of 1958 or being played down as in 1957, the whole doctrinal underpinning of the regime involves the constant identification of the United States and its allies as "the enemy." As long as Peiping is a part of international Communism, this is a force which will continue to direct Chinese power. It cannot be washed away; it dare not be forgotten. Mao is dedicated to the global victory of Communism under Moscow's leadership and this overshadows all secondary problems.*

2. National pride

The Chinese people have been a proud people through their long history, displaying ofttimes an attitude of superiority toward outsiders. The Communist leaders are aware that China was once *the* great power in all Asia, and we must not discount the nationalistic psychology which demands restoration of Chinese leadership. Although China was never a colony like other countries, she was subjected to Western military attacks and unequal treaties in the last century, and Peiping's rulers assure other countries in Asia that they share much in common. The psychology of many intellectuals in Asia demands frequent displays of equal status with the once haughty West, and China's new leaders share this psychology. They are convinced of the necessity of maintaining their new prestige no matter what the sacrifice. For them it is a matter of national face. At the Eighth Party Congress in September 1956, for example, Liu Shao-ch'i pointed to the "victorious war to resist U.S. aggression and aid Korea" and concluded that the "international position of our country has been elevated," giving China "a great power of attraction in international life among all the oppressed nations and exploited peoples."

Two years later at the great anti-U.S. and anti-British mass rally staged in Peiping July 18, 1958, in connection with events in the Middle East, Peiping's mayor and Politburo member Peng Chen stated:

The U.S. Government has now discarded its mask. Before the people of the world it now stands uncov-

---

* For an official statement of the two-camp view of the world issued by the Peiping leadership, see Appendix I.

ered, its imperialist wolfish features clearly revealed, and no amount of pretexts which it may fabricate can in any way hide them. We Chinese people have long perceived the wolfish features of the U.S. imperialists. In our past struggles with U.S. imperialism, we have dealt heavy blows to their aggressive designs and won brilliant victories. We have, moreover, proved to the whole world that the U.S. imperialists, though vicious and seemingly ferocious, are not to be feared. They are only a paper tiger, outwardly strong but internally weak.[77]

The nationalist psychology being exploited by the Chinese Communists is likely to demand further victories as proof not only of equality with Western powers but of the leadership being asserted in Asia. We should not, however, discount the possibility that Chinese national pride and traditional xenophobia may cause real tensions in the alliance with the Soviet "Big Brothers." While Mao with his highly symbolized leadership position may be able to continue Peiping's subordination to Moscow, it may become increasingly difficult for his successors to do so. Soviet leaders have, however, seemingly profited from the Tito experience and have been extremely careful in handling Chinese nationalism and according it a leadership role in Asia.[78] Nevertheless, some refugees of European background who have come to Hong Kong have told of violence displayed against them by Chinese who mistook them for Soviet advisors.

3. The experience of the present leadership

The men ruling in Peiping are not yet old men. More important, they are first generation Communists. Their dedication and fanaticism has been reinforced by their success. They are unlikely to abandon the philosophy and the power system to which they attribute their present strong position. In both internal and external policies and actions they can be expected to utilize the elements of power (discussed above) which have contributed so greatly to their success. Most of these leaders are men with military experience. They are accustomed to command, and this reinforces their Leninist philosophy which views every action in the context of struggle, of warfare and campaigns.

The Chinese leaders have found that following the dictates of Bolshevik expediency has paid off handsomely. They have not hesitated to fabricate and distort facts or to abrogate or break agreements, nor have they shrunk from violence. In their minds it is a necessary part of an implacable struggle. They have produced their own documentation on the liquidation of millions of their fellow countrymen in the name of class war. They fully accept Lenin's 1920 dictum, "Our morality is deduced from the class struggle of the proletariat. . . . Communist morality is the morality which serves this struggle." It is against such a background of the present Peiping leadership that seemingly valid proposals for getting together with them with the hope that they will be "reasonable" must be weighed. They are hardly likely to accept facts which demonstrate that their philosophy is inaccurate, archaic, and intellectually discredited when they believe, as Mao Tse-tung stated at the opening of the Eighth Party Congress on September 15, 1956, "The victories of the revolution and construction in our country are victories of Marxism-Leninism."

4. *The dynamics of totalitarianism*

We still lack adequate explanation of why totalitarian states, especially newly-founded ones, have tended almost without exception to be expansionist. Unfortunately, statements and predictions from Peiping give us ample reason to expect Chinese conformity with the pattern, especially given the two-camp view held. One possible reason lies in the totalitarian necessity of maintaining infallibility and complete monopoly of "truth." This can usually be challenged from the outside, so one after another outside challengers must be eliminated. Top leaders of Mao's regime proudly proclaimed at the 1956 Party Congress that they had not made a single mistake in party line in the past twenty-one years. At the May 1958 meeting they promised ever greater victories in terms of socialist transformation, industrialization, building of state power, and growth of the "camp of peace and democracy."[79]

Another reason for expansion by totalitarian states probably lies in the necessity of having pariahs, external and internal, in order to justify continued harsh measures of dictatorship. The present regime in Peiping has given many indications that it operates under these compulsions of what has been termed the "totalitarian dilemma." To maintain the myth of infallibility it must continue to have substantial victories whether in terms of eliminating internal enemies, of great strides in industrialization and consolidation of power, or of victories over as yet uncontrolled external enemies. Liu Shao-ch'i warned the Party Congress on May 5, 1958 that the Chinese comrades must be prepared for a "fierce life-and-death struggle with the enemy," and to wage "prolonged and repeated struggles against the bourgeois Rightists."

5. Domestic problems

With the start of the new Five Year Plan and the "big leap forward" in 1958 the Chinese were told that they must make even greater sacrifices for victories in industrialization and for the cause of proletarian internationalism. Chou En-lai had put them on notice at the Party Congress on September 16, 1956 that sacrifices were not necessarily for China's national interest alone:

> Being a member of the Socialist Camp, our country has its share of responsibility. We must fulfill this

share of responsibility. We have the obligation to supply needed farm products, pastoral products, mineral ores, raw materials, and certain mechanical equipment and industrial products to the different fraternal countries [i.e. the Communist bloc]. We must try hard to increase production and reduce domestic consumption appropriately, so as to insure the supply of these products.[80]

The USSR may be able to continue the industrial aid to China if its prices are met, but there is serious question whether in view of increasing population pressure the Chinese can, despite collective control, curtail consumption any further in order to meet Soviet prices. More than half of all China's exports have been farm produce. Shortages in 1957 forced a sizeable curtailment in exports compared with 1956. Grain exports were cut almost in half.[81] To the rulers firmly committed to the heavy industrialization of their country and faced with a shortage of agricultural and raw materials, control over or at least access to the surplus areas of Southeast Asia and Taiwan can become an overriding concern. This may help to explain the intense attention which Mao's China is giving to building up its prestige and promoting its goals in that area since the Bandung Conference.

If, given its promises of economic assistance abroad and pledges toward building world Communist power, Pei-ping finds it has over-committed itself, rather than burst the bubble of infallibility it may find it advantageous to be involved in a limited war which could elicit greater sacrifices from a populace stirred up by nationalism. The leadership is fully capable of presenting any outbreak of hostilities as an attack against China. The war in Korea, according to the organ of the Central Committee of the Chinese Communist Party, proved "a great dynamic power which drove forward our national construction programmes in all aspects."[82]

CHAPTER IV

CHINESE COMMUNIST GOALS

Many of the goals of the new Chinese power are implicit in the power structure itself and in the forces directing it. About most of these goals, which have not changed despite changing tactics, the leaders are quite open. Most fit within the framework of the Communist doctrine which dictates an overriding commitment to the expansion of the Communist system. The Chinese have demonstrated with consistency that they are dedicated proletarian internationalists, and their consistent backing of Moscow through the 1956 and 1958 crises in the Communist movement confirmed the statements by the leaders that their choice was irrevocable.

A corollary of this goal is to split and weaken the camp of the enemy, and here, as pointed out above, the paramount concern is to isolate and defeat the United States. The *People's Daily* confirmed this aspect of Peiping's strategy for its readers in June 1958: "Our experience has shown that our revolutionary efforts should be directed toward isolation of major enemies and neutralization of minor ones. If circumstances permit, further efforts should be made to cause the middle-of-the-road nations to emerge from their neutralist stand into forming alliance with us."[83]

Mao's goal of splitting the camp of the enemy has been facilitated by Chinese ability to exploit anti-Westernism in the former colonial areas of Asia and push Lenin's imposed definition that colonialism and imperialism are the offspring of capitalism. Chou En-lai's report on the Bandung Conference to his colleagues in Peiping (May 13, 1955) indicated his Party's calculation that identification with anti-colonialism and accent on racialism would constitute a key item in plans for weakening the camp of the enemy.[84] The editorial in the *People's Daily* of January 4, 1958, hailing the Communist-dominated Afro-Asian Solidarity Conference held in Cairo stated, for example:

> The fact that colonialism is still seriously threatening the national independence, sovereignty and territorial integrity of the countries in Asia and Africa and destroying the freedom and the living conditions of their people is clear to the people of these countries. In Africa especially, millions of people are still under colonialist rule and are existing in extreme poverty and humiliation and are denied their rights. Racial discrimination and persecution prevail there. Many places have been subjected to agony by the colonialists. At the same time, the most vicious colonialists, those of the United States, are frantically carrying out imperialist plots in Asia and Africa, trying to take the place of the old colonial powers and impose their new colonialist yoke on the people of Asia and Africa.[85]

This line has been the cornerstone of Peiping's policy in Asia and Africa from the beginning. Continued growth of neutralism throughout the world (East Europe excepted) has been hailed by Chinese Communist leaders as evidence of weakness and splits within the "imperialist camp." Anti-colonialism and racialism formed the basis on which Mao's colleagues pushed their interpretation of the Middle East crises of 1956 and 1958.

In 1954, Peiping attempted to drive a wedge between Britain and the United States by adopting a somewhat conciliatory policy toward the British. In this way they hoped to exploit differences on China policy between London and Washington. Beginning in 1958, however, the Chinese attitude hardened, and apparently the Communist rulers decided they had more to gain by adopting a threatening attitude toward both powers. With the year of the "great leap forward" accompanied by claims of "astounding successes" Peiping launched a simultaneous three-pronged offensive in the Far East. Two prongs of the drive were political—one against the British in Hong Kong and another against Japan—and the third military—a build-up and attack against the off-shore islands of Matsu and Quemoy held by the United States-backed Nationalists. Unfortunately the attention of the non-Communist world was focused on the crisis in the Middle East and on military activities in the Taiwan Strait area, and the two political prongs of the offensive and their coordination with the military prong passed almost unnoticed.

The political offensive against the British in Hong Kong which began in May and June was obviously well planned. In connection with British attempts to curtail political activities within private schools in the Crown Colony, the schools were forbidden to fly the Chinese Communist flag. Violations in connection with Labor Day (May 1) resulted in official intervention. The following month a propaganda campaign of protest was launched in the Communist press both in Hong Kong and on the mainland. Labor unions and leftist groups held meetings and passed resolutions expressing their "unanimous discontent and indignation." Similar protests and demonstrations in July forced a decision to cancel an International Trade Fair which had been scheduled for August 8 by the Kowloon Chamber of Commerce. Meanwhile the Chinese Communists began flooding the Hong Kong market with low priced goods in an economic pressure campaign. The deportation of Parker Tu, principal of a middle school on August 8, for violation of regulations brought a long denunciation of the British authorities in the Peiping *People's Daily*. On August 26, three days after the shelling of Quemoy began, violence erupted over the closing of the

Chung Hua Middle School, and for several days while mainland newspapers recounted British "atrocities," protest demonstrations were staged. In an official note delivered to the
British charge d'affaires in Peiping the following day the
Chinese Communists demanded "that the British Government and Hong Kong British authorities immediately stop
their provocations against the Chinese people."* The British
were instructed to "make a speedy reply."[86]

Another major goal of the Peiping regime is to establish clearly Chinese leadership in Asia, not only in terms of
anti-imperialism, but as pointed out above, as a model for
achieving power against the West. The Chinese leaders now
feel that they are well on their way to achieving this goal.
They have been especially anxious to make leadership felt
vis-à-vis Japan, industrially the most advanced power in Asia
and a power over which they wish to assert their new prestige
for historical as well as nationalistic reasons.

The political offensive against Japan in 1958 was
mainly connected with a trade agreement negotiated in Peiping by private Japanese groups. The Chinese Communists
had already utilized Japan's crucial need for trade to insist on
a revision of Japanese immigration laws to eliminate the
necessity of fingerprinting those who stayed in Japan for less
than a year; the revision was approved by the Japanese cabinet
on January 31. During the following month there was great
debate in Japan over certain provisions of the draft trade
agreement and an attached memorandum. These provided
inter alia the stationing of a permanent Chinese Communist
trade mission in Japan, the equivalent of diplomatic immunity for its unlimited number of representatives, the right
of the mission to fly the Communist Chinese flag on its build-

---

* For documents dealing with the Chung Hua Middle School incident and Communist pressure against the British in Hong Kong, see
Appendix III.

ing, guarantees of security for personnel, and the right to use secret codes. The Japanese Government which recognizes the Republic of China on Taiwan, could obviously not agree to such conditions. On February 22, the ruling Liberal-Democratic Party of Premier Nobusuke Kishi announced that it could not go along with the pact as it then stood. The following day Chinese Communist Premier Chou En-lai delivered a bitter denunciation of Kishi.[87] The private groups involved in the negotiations with Peiping declared they would sign the trade agreement anyway—which they did on March 5. The *People's Daily* immediately insisted that the Japanese Government must insure the implementation of the agreement.[88] Following much debate in Japan during which the Kishi Government was subjected to pressures from all sides—including the breaking off of trade talks by the Chinese Nationalists in Taiwan—Peiping finally disavowed the pact on April 13, when it became apparent that the Japanese Government would not capitulate.[89].

The next development was the so-called Nagasaki flag incident. At 4:20 P.M. on May 2, a 31-year-old Japanese draftsman tore down a flag hanging in a small room in a Nagasaki department store where a display of Chinese Communist stamps was being held. The Japanese press carried no account of the incident. Three days later a Japanese news agency reported from China that Peiping took a very grave view of the incident and the Chinese People's Government intended to file a protest with the Japanese Foreign Ministry against the "release of the two Japanese who had insulted the flag of Communist China flying from the roof of the Nagasaki department store." These distortions of the facts of the case indicated an incident was in the making. (This was the very time of flag incidents in Hong Kong.) By May 7, New China News Agency dispatches in the Japanese newspapers were asserting that the incident was "inspired by the Chiang Kai-shek group and the Kishi clique." Japanese firms doing business with Communist China cabled apologies for the incident.[90] That same day armed Chinese vessels seized 170 Japanese fishermen off the coast of China.[91] On May 9, Peiping's Foreign Minister Ch'en Yi delivered a bitter attack against Kishi, accusing him of openly conniving in the Nagasaki flag incident, asserting that his attitude did not represent the desires of the Japanese people, and supporting the Japanese Socialist Party which was in favor of restoring normal diplomatic relations between Tokyo and Peiping.[92] The following day (May 10) Communist China cut off all trade with Japan.

In view of the oncoming Japanese elections on May 22, many people in Japan regarded this as crude interference in their internal affairs. Kishi's main opposition was not from the Communists, but the Socialists, who stood for a shift away from the solid alliance with the West toward some form of "neutralism." Peiping evidently overplayed its hand, for the Kishi Government was returned to power by a much bigger margin than expected in an election in which more than 70 per cent of the eligible voters participated.[93]

Following this rebuff, Peiping continued with further pressures on Japan in early June (at the same time they began organizing demonstrations against the British in Hong Kong). On June 4, for example, the Chinese Red Cross notified Japan that it would cease giving aid to Japanese wives of Chinese who wished to return to Japan for visits. Their telegram stated: "Since the Kishi cabinet remains hostile to China, the Chinese Red Cross will suspend for a while its assistance."[94] A week later the Chinese Fishery Association notified Japan that it was dropping the fishing pact which had been signed in 1955. It told the Japanese fishermen:

> The Kishi government of your country, courting favor with the Chiang Kai-shek clique in Taiwan, has adopted a blatant policy of extreme unfriendliness and hostility toward the 600 million Chinese

people and has thus completely destroyed the basis of friendly cooperation with fishery circles of China and Japan. In these circumstances, we regret to inform you that the extension of the Sino-Japanese fishery agreement is out of the question.[95]

The need for trade made the Japanese businessmen acutely conscious of Chinese Communist products, especially cotton cloth, which during the summer began to invade many of the markets which the Japanese had developed in Southeast Asia.[96] Some Japanese visitors to the Chinese mainland reported being given the cold shoulder by the Chinese people in a manner which could not have been sheer accident.[97] Individual Japanese made inquiries about what could be done to break the trade deadlock. Finally, on August 29 (six days after the shelling of Quemoy started and two days after the Chinese Communists presented their demands to the British), the report of Tadataka Sata, a high-ranking member of the Socialist Party just back from Peiping, hit the Japanese press. Sata's outline of the Mao regime's conditions for resumption of trade flabbergasted the Japanese. In brief, Peiping's six-point proposal to the Japanese was:

1. The Kishi Government must stop all speeches and actions which regard Communist China as an enemy and guarantee against their recurrence.
2. The Kishi Government must immediately stop the plot aiming at the creation of "two Chinas."
3. The Kishi Government must guarantee not again to impair normal relations between Japan and Communist China.
4. Regarding the Nagasaki flag incident the Kishi Government should
   a. Dispatch a formal delegate to the scene of the incident to hoist there a national flag of Communist China.
   b. Punish the culprit with a punishment com-

       patible with the offense of insulting the flag
       of a friendly power.

   c. Send a formal mission to Peiping to express
       regrets for the national flag incident.

5. To guarantee against the plot for "two Chinas,"
    the Kishi Government should issue the following
    statement: "The Japanese Government, aspiring
    for the restoration of normal relations with the
    Government of the People's Republic of China
    will make all efforts for that purpose."

6. When the above five conditions have been met to
    the fullest extent, the Japanese Government may
    send a delegation to Peiping to discuss future
    problems.[98]

What amounted to an ultimatum from Peiping and the furor it created in the Japanese press and in Tokyo political circles—like the Hong Kong prong of the Chinese Communist 1958 offensive—passed almost unnoticed in the West where attention was focused on Quemoy. Judging from Japanese reaction, Mao's regime had underestimated Japanese national pride and the stability and continuity of the Japanese political system. The spokesmen of the Liberal-Democratic Party wondered, "Was Tadataka Sata in his senses when he wrote his report?"[99] Two factions within the Socialist Party coldly branded the Sata visit to Communist China "a failure" and urged that the Party formulate its policy on China independent of the report.[100] Other observers pointed out that neither trade nor the flag incident was the real issue. These were rather part of a larger drive to break the Japanese-United States alliance; encourage neutralism in Japan; eliminate American bases in Japan, Okinawa and Taiwan; and force the withdrawal of United States forces from the Western Pacific.[101] Joint statements by Chinese Communist leaders and members of the Japanese delegation present in Peiping

for the October 1, 1958 celebrations and parade indicated
that such observations were not far from the mark.[102]*

The Chinese Communist political offensive against
Japan offers a vivid example of the ability of totalitarian
regimes to take advantage of the divisions and multiple interests in the free societies with which they deal. This is an
item to which we shall return later. The emphasis here is on
the intensity of Communist China's effort to call the tune in
Asia, especially over Japan.

A key Chinese Communist goal is to bring all Chinese
citizens within a single framework of control and influence.
This includes especially the remaining opposition government on Taiwan. Mao's regime made extensive preparations
for the "liberation" of Taiwan in late 1949 and the spring of
1950, but called off the effort.[103] With the Communist aggression in Korea and the interposition of the United States
Seventh Fleet by President Truman in June 1950, the
Republic of China was protected by United States power.
From 1954 to 1957 Peiping attempted to win Taiwan by
peaceful subversion, even offering a high position and pardon
to Chiang Kai-shek, whom they had formerly condemned as
a "war criminal." During May and June 1957, when Mao
encouraged critics on the mainland to speak up, there was
ample evidence that Taiwan represented far more of an
alternate symbol to Communist totalitarianism than the outside world had realized. In student demonstrations, which
occurred in every mainland province, banners were carried
proclaiming "Welcome back, President Chiang Kai-shek."[104]
Mao's subsequent reversion to harsh Stalinist methods in an
"anti-Rightist campaign" probably eliminated any hopes,
however slim, for peaceful accommodation with the Chinese
Nationalists. Following the return of Peiping's top military

---

* For a document indicating the serious tone of Peiping's threats
against Japan see Appendix IV.

leaders from Moscow in December 1957, the Communists stepped up military preparations opposite Taiwan and the off-shore islands. The internal Chinese Communist press renewed its campaign of vilification against the United States and "the Chiang Kai-shek clique."

In July 1958, while Peiping was leading in a seeming worldwide Communist competition to denounce Tito and carrying on its political offensive against Japan and Hong Kong, the Chinese Communists warned: "We solemnly declare again that Taiwan must be liberated and that the intrigue to create 'two Chinas' shall not pass. Any illusion entertained on this question will certainly be smashed by the facts."[105] Chinese people on the mainland were reminded that "before and after the Korean armistice, the United States, by resorting to the most outrageous and sanguinary measures, had detained 48,000 Chinese and Korean prisoners of war and so far has refused to give an accounting for them. The Chinese and Korean people will never forget this blood debt and will settle it with the United States without fail."[106] Broadcasts directed toward Taiwan in early August warned of impending "liberation" for the people there. Peiping told the Chinese on Taiwan, "The Chiang Kai-shek clique depends on the United States, which as we have said is merely a 'paper tiger,' and is not dependable. Furthermore, in the present world situation the position of the West is inferior to that of the East, and the strength of the imperialist camp is definitely much weaker than that of the socialist camp."[107]

The military prong of Communist China's offensive in the Far East was thrust into full operation with the start of intense artillery bombardment of Quemoy and Matsu on August 23. The subsequent protracted period of crisis put pressures on free world alliances—especially between Britain and the United States and between the Republic of China and the United States. Concentration of the violence on the off-shore islands led to disagreement between allies as well as within the United States as to whether those islands could be separated as an issue of the fate of Taiwan and the Pescadores. Arguments over Quemoy and Matsu tended to obscure the relationship of the bombardment to Peiping's overall policy and pose of unbeatable strength and the coordination with the political offensive in the Far East. Moscow gave full support to Peiping's militant stand. In a letter to President Eisenhower on September 7—which the United States President returned as too abusive—Nikita Khrushchev warned that "An attack on the People's Republic of China . . . is an attack on the Soviet Union." The Soviet premier stated: "There can be no stable peace in the Far East until the American naval forces are withdrawn from the Taiwan Strait, until the American soldiers are recalled home from Taiwan."[108]

Peiping used a well-timed combination of political and military tactics to widen fissures between Washington and Taipei and to sow defeatism among the Chinese Nationalists. On September 30, for example, Secretary of State Dulles, in response to domestic pressure, especially over the question of the off-shore islands, indicated in a news conference the possibility of a more flexible United States approach to the crisis. This was in contrast with the former resolute policy he had maintained, and the move caused consternation in Taiwan. One week later, on October 6, when the Chinese Communists announced a seven-day suspension of their bombardment, Peiping's Minister of National Defense Peng Teh-huai quickly exploited this sign of wavering in his message to the Chinese Nationalists: "The day will certainly come when the Americans will abandon you. Do you not believe it? History will bear witness to it. The clue is already there in the statement made by Dulles on September 30. In the last analysis," he said, "the American imperialists are our common enemy."[109]

In an interview with Canadian correspondent Gerald Clark in Peiping on November 1, 1958, when the Communists

were demonstrating their ability to call the turn by bombard-
ing the off-shore islands only on alternate days, Foreign Minister Chen Yi declared that this "punitive shelling" was "to
enlighten Chiang Kai-shek with a sense of national duty and
tell him not to rely on a foreign insurance company which is
no good." Chen repeated the Communist refusal to consider
the off-shore islands as a separate issue, asserting that Taiwan,
the Pescadores, Quemoy, and Matsu "must be liberated as a
whole" and that the Americans must withdraw from the Taiwan area.[110]

Peiping's three-pronged offensive in 1958 and the
general threatening and self-confidence stance in foreign
policy probably served several ends. Documents from the
mainland indicate that Mao Tse-tung was utilizing external
crisis to extract greater efforts and sacrifices from the Chinese
people for the "great leap forward" which would insure that
the "East wind prevails over the West wind." Certainly the
external offensive served to distract attention from the attack
on the Chinese family and the tensions involved in the creation of the communes. If by the military action directed towards Taiwan the Communists could prove America would
back down or compromise in face of threatened large-scale
hostilities, Peiping's prestige would be high indeed. The free
world alliance structure could be seriously undermined.
Propaganda directed toward the Nationalists showed that the
Communist leaders confidently expected from violence the
results which the soft line from 1954 to 1957 had failed to
achieve.

But in terms of gaining the undisputed allegiance of
all Chinese and coping with their "totalitarian dilemma"
there was probably another more compelling reason for the
military attempt to eliminate Nationalist resistance. This was
pointed out in October, 1958 by Michael Lindsay (Lord
Lindsay of Birker) who had served as interpreter from the
Attlee mission to mainland China in 1954 and has close per-

sonal knowledge of the top Communist leaders. Lord Lindsay referred to the possibility:

> . . . that the Peiping regime feels that the Taiwan regime, as a living example of "Free China" is a real danger to it and . . . it might, therefore, be ready to take considerable risks to destroy it.

The identification of the Taiwan regime with Chiang Kai-shek has led many people to overlook the big changes that have taken place on the island since 1949. A very successful land reform program has been carried out. Rice production is one-third higher than the best attained under Japanese rule and the average peasant on Taiwan has about twice the income of his opposite number on the mainland. Industrialization may not be so fast as on the mainland but it has made great progress both in heavy and consumer goods industries. Elementary education is now almost universal and higher education has been expanded.

Civil liberties are restricted on Taiwan, but there is nothing like the police-state atmosphere of the mainland and strong criticism of the Government can be published. . . . Local government works through elected mayors and elected councils up to the Provincial Assembly, and the Kuomintang has built up a strong local organization in Taiwan.

The Peiping leaders may, accordingly, have very good reasons for wanting to end a practical demonstration that a different type of Chinese regime can carry out agrarian reform which gives better results than collectivization, can secure quite rapid economic progress without the forced austerity which goes with industrialization under communism, and can do all this while allowing a much greater degree of freedom and a much greater degree of actual popular control. The increasing proportion of Overseas Chinese students going to universities in Taiwan shows that Taiwan is competing effectively with the mainland in an important field.[111]

The continuance of an alternate Chinese regime on Taiwan prevents the Chinese Communists from gaining control of the 12 to 14 million Overseas Chinese. Mao and his colleagues are well aware that the overthrow of the Manchu rule in China was financed and plotted among the Overseas Chinese. They know of the great financial power of the Overseas Chinese in practically every country of Southeast Asia, and they are acutely aware of the tremendous boost in power that an undivided allegiance among these compatriots throughout Southeast Asia would give them in any future plans for "liberation" there. Observers in Hong Kong noted that the creation of the "people's communes" was seriously damaging Peiping's attraction among the Overseas Chinese.[112] Thus there was added reason for a Communist willingness to run frightening risks to take over Taiwan.

Communist plans for the Overseas Chinese were spelled out in detail in a broadcast by Ho Hsiang-ning, Chief Commissioner of Overseas Chinese Affairs, on New Year's Day 1950. She told the Chinese in Southeast Asia that their duty was (1) to form a people's democratic united front with local people, (2) to resist the influence and power of Europeans and Americans in their places of residence, and (3) to act as the "outer circle" of the vanguard of international Communism! In the last few years, the overt line to the Overseas Chinese has called for them to become good citizens in the host state. But covert organization, activity and propaganda have continued.[113]

One other goal of the Chinese Communists deserves mention: their determination to convince the world, and especially their neighbors in Asia, that they are on the side of history. They utilize every resource at their disposal to sell the defeatism which acceptance of this doctrine breeds. Every concession wrung from the West by threat and vituperation is presented as further proof that the *inevitable* victory rests with the Communist camp. Liu Shao-ch'i's closing words to his lengthy speech (the length of his speeches is frequently a test of and testament to party discipline) to the 1956 Party Congress were: "Our great cause of Socialism will definitely triumph! No force in the world can stop us from winning victory." In his equally long speech to the meeting in May 1958, he referred again to "The inevitable victory of our cause."

The foregoing resumé of some of the goals directing the power of Mao's China has made extensive use of official statements by top Communist leaders. They indicate a pattern of thought and action, an operational code, which has been a consistent feature in the policies of Mao and his cohorts for more than three decades. All too frequently this operational code is overlooked or forgotten in the non-Communist world when the official line for external consumption concentrates on such momentary tactics as united front or peaceful co-existence. This operational code is a feature of Communist China which is unlikely to change while the current leadership is in power. A close reading of every important policy statement indicates that the Chinese Communists have never shown any intention of budging from their overall dedication to world revolution. They plan continued expansion and revolutionary war in Asia, and for this purpose they may be expected to exploit to the fullest those advantages which have given them their new power status in Asia. This is the prime consideration which must be taken into account by those who must deal with Peiping in the years ahead, years that promise continuing struggle.

CHAPTER V

THE "ORGANIZATIONAL WEAPON" IN ASIA

In view of mainland China's build-up and parades of armed might it should be obvious that Communist leaders never discount the possibility of open armed violence. It is this possibility which has caused a state of military alert along China's borders since Mao came to power. Like Lenin and Stalin, Mao has always favored violence. According to him, "The central task and the highest form of revolution is the armed seizure of political power. Revolution is solving problems by war." The preponderance of military men in high positions in the mainland regime is a sure indication that the Chinese Reds subscribe to the Leninist view of the relationship between war and politics. Mao told his comrades in Yenan in 1938, "Politics is war without bloodshed, and war is politics with bloodshed."[114]

Overt violence, such as the Western powers faced in Korea and has existed in the Taiwan Strait may not, however, be the main type of struggle on which Peiping will rely in Asia in the years ahead. The actions of the Chinese in recent years have shown that they appreciate only too well the unwillingness and inability of other nations to understand their doctrine of permanent conflict. It would be absurd to assume that the Chinese Communist leadership would fail to take advantage of the West's tendency to regard peace as a normal state or fail to exploit all advantages they possess to make advances on the political and propaganda fronts. Such advances could prove every bit as devastating for the free world as those won by open warfare. It is here the possibility that the Chinese Communists have developed a new dimension of power in terms of an "organizational weapon," to use Philip Salznik's apt phrase, takes on special significance.[115] Perhaps this significance is best brought out in historical perspective.

From the 16th through the 19th century, Western influence and control was extended over most of the world. Although there is much disagreement concerning the relative weight of the various reasons for this expansion, there is general agreement that it was made possible by the West's relative monopoly in organizing non-human power, *i.e.*, technology, for its ends. This basis of superiority made possible, for example, the rule over millions in India by a few thousand British. But with the gradual disappearance of the monopoly, old colonial empires have begun to break up. In Asia, Japan was the first power to score a break-through in mobilizing non-human power. From the beginning of the present century, she was able to sow the seeds for further challenge by colonial peoples in the East. With the exception of highly destructive weapons which the West is hesitant to use, it must now face the fact that its basis of superiority in Asia is rapidly becoming non-existent.

In some cases influence and control is still maintained through a preponderance of mechanized military might which continues important, as for example, armed Soviet suppression of Hungary's bid for freedom in 1956 or the armed break-up of the East German riots following the death of Stalin. But, with respect to the expansion of Chinese influence and control the explanation cannot be made entirely in such conventional terms. Statements emanating from Peiping indicate that the leaders there believe they have indeed developed a new dimension of power by turning attention back to the human element of power. They are confident that through their monolithic organization and control over formerly inconsequential masses they have a new basis of superiority. They assert that they intend to exploit it to the fullest in pushing to the final victory.

The internal implications of the organizational weapon as a new dimension of power have already been noted. With regard to the expansion of Chinese Communist influence and control abroad without overt military attack, there are two general fields where Peiping may be expected to exploit its organizational weapon. In both fields the free world is called upon to cope with an already well-developed strategy for the utilization of this organizational power. The first field lies in pushing the strategy for seizure of power in economically underdeveloped areas primarily by covert methods which the Chinese Communists developed through their own experience and have since been polishing and perfecting. The second lies in utilizing their own total power structure to promote Communist goals internationally and to expand areas of influence, especially in Asia, by overt methods. This second has relied primarily on the lessons of Soviet experience. In both cases, the organizational weapon is the key.[116]

SEIZING POWER IN ASIA

There has been much heated debate as to whether the strategy for seizure of power was an original creation of Mao Tse-tung or whether Lenin and Stalin were the formulators. This is a matter of relatively small import in the present context. What matters is that a well-formulated strategy does now exist. It has been successful, and it is being applied elsewhere in Asia with flexibility and effectiveness. It is within the framework of this strategy that the Chinese Communists regard their revolution as the classical type for areas in Asia where the masses are as yet unorganized, inarticulate and unsophisticated.

Certainly the Soviets played a role in developing many of the prerequisite bases for the evolution of the strategy. These would include techniques for organizing and training native Communist cadres from the target areas who will be dedicated servants of a centralized structure built upon the monolithic Communist doctrine. This creation of an élite corps of revolutionaries bound into a tightly-knit group capable of intensive propaganda and subversion constitutes the first stage of the strategy. The second stage starts when this revolutionary élite returns to their home territory and launches an attrition-type program of guerrilla operations, sabotage, propaganda, infiltration and expansion of their own organization by inclusion of discontented groups in the society. This stage is calculated to take advantage of the usually unpopular nature of regimes in underdeveloped areas. It forces them to spend meager resources on military forces to cope with the guerrillas thus preventing the very measures for social improvement which the propagandists begin to demand with increasing effectiveness. The fact that it takes a minimum of twenty formally organized and equipped troops to deal with one guerrilla (for the British in Malaya it required up to 40 for ten years) makes even a very small Communist force effective. In the underdeveloped areas it becomes an easy matter to undermine administrative integrity and efficiency and purposefully to foster corruption in order to decry it.

In the third stage, the revolutionaries emerge as formally constituted popular parties which claim that the violence has been the result of oppressed people giving vent to their grievances. These parties demand a role in the government in the name of the interests of the "people" whom they claim to represent. Often by this time their organization is so strong and extensive that the weakened governments are forced to accept the idea of coalition or united front. Meanwhile when possible a territorial base of operations has been built up (Mao deems this essential). The inclusion of these parties in international Communist conferences and organizations as true representatives of their people gives them added stature. Any attempt by outside powers to help the weakened local regimes in their predicament can easily be exploited in terms of the re-extension of colonial rule to help corrupt regimes oppress the people.

If, after full utilization of the many advantages created for the revolutionary party during this stage, the regime still refuses to budge, then the strategy enters its fourth stage—open warfare on a territorial basis. By this time the local administration has probably been thoroughly infiltrated, a fairly easy accomplishment in such politically unsophisticated areas. It is probably so weak and in such ill repute, and the people are so tired of violence that the outcome of the resultant civil war is a foregone conclusion. Issues and forces are far from clear-cut, and the Communists have emerged as the most consistent champions of local aspirations. Inhabitants rush to join the winning side. Victorious Communist forces take full control, their total organizational power is imposed, and the area is immediately sealed off from the non-Communist world.

Such a brief outline can hardly be more than a caricature of the strategy which has been and continues to be applied throughout many areas in Asia. There are in actual practice no such clear divisions between stages. Techniques and issues vary from country to country. This is, however, the general outline given by Ho Chi Minh when he said that his triumph in Vietnam was based on the successful experience of the Chinese Communists under the guidance of the Soviet Union.

Certain factors, which remain constant throughout this struggle, deserve passing mention. In the first place, it should be noted that the strategy places a premium on armed revolution. Second, there is consistent consultation and coordination with the Communist bloc so that local revolutionaries will always be able to present themselves as representatives of a great world force whose power cannot be denied. But the actual burden of work is carried by organized nationals of the country involved. Third, no matter what the fortunes of the revolutionaries at a particular moment, there is never any relaxation in the effort to recruit, train, and organize new members. Finally, every local problem and bit of opposition is brought within the two-world-camp interpretation so that the ever-growing strength of the organizational and propaganda effort can be used to demonstrate that victory for the "camp of peace, socialism, and democracy" is inevitable. This enables the Communists to exploit the issues of national independence and colonialism even where they do not exist. The real basis for their confidence in this strategy, however, rests on the Communists' calculation that they can be the first to get the masses in such areas effectively organized.

The non-Communist world has been coping with this strategy of aggression by subversion for a number of years in the Asian areas adjacent to China, especially in Southeast Asia. The effectiveness of the second stage of guerrilla warfare and propaganda was illustrated by the fact that the fate of many of the newly independent states of Southeast Asia was in doubt between 1949 and 1954. The viability of some of these governments at present, in contrast with the earlier period, indicates that there has been some progress in meeting the threat. But such limited progress as has been made to date has rested in part on an ability to depart from conventional patterns, to develop counter-strategies of organization and to tackle some of the problems of ignorance, poverty, and gross inequality, especially in land tenure. It has also rested upon outside willingness and ability to assist new governments in building necessary military power to cope with the insurgents.

But the Communist strategy directed against the underdeveloped areas is a powerful one, and in many respects there is still a failure to recognize that the conventional answers of economic and military aid are inadequate so long as the local people lack organization for the pursuit of their own goals. This could prove a long-run tragedy in view of apparent Chinese intentions to continue a method which they have every reason to believe is still effective. Indeed, in some countries in Southeast Asia, tensions between the Overseas Chinese and the native inhabitants and divisions among the Overseas Chinese themselves have played almost as great a role in preventing Peiping from being successful as some of the positive steps taken by the free world.

In some of the critical areas of Southeast Asia the Communists shifted to the third stage of the strategy following the Bandung Conference (April 1955). In line with the current tack of world Communism in Asia and Africa they are now pushing for peaceful co-existence and coalition but at the same time maintaining a vigorous anti-Western tone. The power of local organizations is being put behind an all-out propaganda drive for a united front within each country against the "imperialists" or possibly in favor of neutralism which is regarded as a first step away from the West. In this drive China's new prestige and power position are of immeasurable help. Here is where the second general field for the Chinese exploitation of their new basis of superiority through organization enters in; that is, in their conduct of foreign relations. And here again we are enjoined to face the possibility that conventional answers and actions are inadequate.

CULTURAL COLD WAR

It is possible that the overt aspects of China's use of her organizational weapon in the international arena may prove even more effective than the covert methods of aggression by subversion. In the conduct of relations between states there are certain opportunities available to totalitarian regimes which do not obtain for others. Regimes like that on the Chinese mainland are obviously less limited by public opinion. Their monopoly over internal communications means that they do not have to accommodate to division of opinion within their own home territories, and further, foreign states are denied equal access in terms of presenting their point of view. Monolithic organization and control enables the presentation of a complete solidarity in backing any of their negotiators, and thus when spokesmen of the Peiping government state that "the Chinese people" demand a particular item, there is little doubt of their ability to mobilize full strength for the support of that demand.

Chinese Communist leaders have demonstrated they have been able to calculate such advantages and utilize them effectively. Like other totalitarian states their use of blandishment in promoting their foreign policy goals has proved fairly successful. They will not hesitate to engage in small or medium-scale military operations in order to drive a hard diplomatic bargain or to alarm and split the free world where the desire for peace is genuine. It is necessary to remind ourselves repeatedly of the preponderant importance of military power in the context of Asia and the fact that the Chinese Communists parade and use their military power in such a way that it never escapes the attention of weaker neighbors. That the Peiping leaders themselves understand the impact of their military strength has been made clear all too frequently. For example, their offers of "volunteers" to Egypt in 1956 and to Indonesia in 1958 were well calculated to remind others of their military power in being. In his report on the Korean War to the Eighth Party Congress on September 18, 1956, Peng Te-huai stated:

> Our efforts have guaranteed the security of the Korean Democratic People's Republic and the

northeastern part of our country, and have also proved that the number one imperialist army of the world can be defeated, demonstrated the great strength of the Chinese people, heightened the National respect of our people, and have also given encouragement to the people throughout the world in their struggle for peace and opposition to war.

That this factor is of some concern to China's smaller neighbors was evidenced in an editorial reaction in the Burmese newspaper *The Nation* to the Chinese Communist invasion there on a limited scale in 1956:

In the midst of countless problems with which our country has had to contend, we have had thrust upon us a major crisis in the shape of Red Chinese aggression. . . . Of all the countries in southeast Asia, Burma has tried the hardest to keep well in with Communist China, and yet it is from that country that the new calamity has come. It is enough to make the politicians groan. Short of abject surrender, what more does China expect from Burma?[117]

(It is worth noting that the China-Burma border issue remains unsettled.) Surely here is an important reason why Communist China has been able to carry so much weight in its foreign relations. But this is stating the obvious.

There is, however, another aspect of Communist diplomacy in Asia which is less obvious and does not seem to be getting the same amount of attention in terms of analyzing it and coping with it, an item which is frequently referred to by the term "cultural diplomacy" or "people's diplomacy." The Peiping regime has drawn upon Soviet experience and developments in this field to create an organized systematic weapon for their struggle against the West. The manner in which this weapon is being used to promote the solidarity of the Communist bloc and to divide the outside world makes the term *cultural cold war* a more apt description.[118] This cultural cold war is especially effective in Asia because of the emotional residue of anti-Westernism and racial sensitivities which can be exploited there. Statements from such Peiping leaders as Premier Chou En-lai indicate that they regard this new dimension of diplomacy as one of their most formidable weapons and that they plan to exploit it thoroughly for the pursuit of world-wide Communist victory.

Heretofore, we have tended to treat the cultural cold war carried on by the Communist countries only with respect to some of its isolated external manifestations such as propaganda, front organizations, and guided tours. But it is, in fact, an integrated organizational weapon, fully representative of centralized Communist power.

Thus, before discussing some of the specific items involved it is probably desirable to point out the justification for treating this as an integrated system capable of being encompassed by one term. In the first place, cultural cold war is directed almost exclusively toward full utilization of activities which have not normally played any significant role in the relations among states. Communist states have been the first to reach out and embrace foreign scholars, musicians, athletes, businessmen, artists and others and make their activities a matter of state concern in foreign relations. Second, the almost exclusive focus of this type of operation is on groupings which in free societies remain beyond the pale of governmental concern and control but which are nevertheless most influential. Communist leaders, therefore, make a calculated attempt to exploit the multi-centered nature of free societies. Finally, by bringing such groupings into association with their opposite numbers within the Communist state whose activities *are* organized and controlled, the leadership hopes to make them serve its own ends. In other words, the Chinese Communist regime is attempting, as in the case of covert organization of formerly insignificant masses in Asia, to be the first to organize such groupings and give them an intimate and exploitable relationship to the centralized leadership of Peiping.[119]

The conferences, delegations, exhibitions, festivals, athletic contests, and guided tours involved in the Chinese conduct of cultural cold war are for the most part under the direction of the Chinese People's Society for Cultural Relations with Foreign Countries, the counterpart of VOKS in the USSR. This organization sees that visitors to Communist China get the best of hospitality. They are given a feeling of importance through conferences and interviews with Chinese leaders. Even the most cynical are swayed by the organized kindnesses showered upon them and the parades of people and glowing figures presented by their hosts. The busy schedules arranged for the visitors and the fact that few of them have any sound knowledge of China or the Chinese language make it difficult for them to get any facts and figures except those on government handouts. The attention they receive in the Chinese press gratifies many, and it serves to convince the Chinese people internally that the important people in the world have accepted and favor the Communist regime. The prodigious amounts of time and money spent on entertaining visitors is testament to the importance attached to this aspect of cold war strategy by the Mao regime.[120]

When they return to their home countries the visitors become one of the best sources for Chinese propaganda. The figures which they cite agree with those published officially by the Peiping authorities thus seeming to sustain the reliability of the latter. The guests do not wish to seem ungrateful to hosts who have treated them so magnificently. Their own people tend to believe their glowing reports of accomplishment and progress in China. Outside of China they become enthusiastic members of Chinese Friendship associations which are organized locally by their own people. These associations then sponsor visits by leading Chinese figures, distribute Chinese Communist propaganda, and show Communist films. The fact that leading statesmen and popular figures from Asia—such as Indonesian President Sukarno, Indian Premier Nehru, Burma's U Nu, and Cambodia's Prince Sihanouk—have also been to the same places and seen the same people in China helps to promote the prestige and authority of the less important visitors. The identification with and interest in Red China becomes a major source of self-gratification and prestige for the lesser lights in their homelands.

The result of such a general program, all too briefly outlined, has been that the Chinese Communists have been able to build up a tremendous support throughout Asia and other areas in the free world; they have been able to make others use their terminology and interpretations of world events, though frequently unwittingly; and they have succeeded in obscuring many of the realities and shortcomings of their police state. Evidence of the success of Peiping's cultural cold war is to be found in the fact that the combined eloquence and weight of their proponents overseas was apparently able to drown out the cries of the Chinese who rose to denounce the Communist regime in May and June 1957. Or again, few people in the free world heard the details of opposition, renewed public executions, failures, and oppression revealed by two Yugoslav correspondents in *Borba* and *Politika* in June 1958.[121] There seemed to be more fascination and interest in the reports of those who had enjoyed a guided tour.

Of course, the Chinese are not original here. It must be remembered that the Soviets demonstrated the effectiveness of cultural cold war before World War II. Some of the most glowing and enthusiastic accounts came out of the USSR during the period of collectivization with its liquidation of the kulaks and the following purges. This was also a period when some optimists were accepting Soviet claims and figures as generally reliable. The key to the effectiveness of the Communist strategy is organization, and the most significant aspect is the fact that nationals of the target areas are organized to carry it on.

Indications of the successes which the Chinese Communists have already scored in Asia through the waging of cultural cold war are only too abundant. For example, early in its history the Peiping regime was able to derive greater benefit from the shipment of half a million tons of grain to India in 1951 and 1952, under tightly bargained inter-governmental sales agreements, than the United States was able to derive from the shipment during the same period of almost four million tons at far below the going market price. In India the branches of the Sino-Indian friendship association are, by legal fiction, groups representative of the Indian people. They therefore do not come under regulations applied to the dissemination of foreign propaganda and can freely circulate Chinese Communist publications and show movies made on the Chinese mainland. The United States and other countries in the free world, on the other hand, have few locally organized groups to present their views, and lose such advantages. India has proved an especially vulnerable target for Peiping's organizational weapon.

In Asia, the ability of Mao's China to play on prejudices as well as local aspirations is reinforced by the emphasis on culture. This emphasis is used to undermine the effectiveness and support for non-Communist military assistance and alliances which are presented as evidence that the capitalist world is bent on war. In a similar manner economic aid is undercut when Communist-led cultural groups portray it as a new and more dangerous form of imperialism.

Unfortunately, even some astute students of foreign affairs have been led to doubt the value of military and economic aid policies and have failed to note the crucial need to provide the organizational underpinning to assure the success of these important aspects of non-Communist security programs abroad. The importance and validity of aid programs, which utilize some of the obvious assets of the more industrially advanced nations of the West, are not in doubt because of Communist successes. These successes merely highlight the fact that aid without organizational backing is wasted. This is why, in terms of foreign policy goals, it can be legitimately questioned, for example, whether the more than half a billion dollars in economic assistance extended by the United States to India since 1951 can begin to compare in effectiveness to the cultural strategy carried on by Peiping in the same period at a comparatively cheap price. Chou En-lai hailed the transfer of Egypt's recognition from the Nationalist Government to the Communist in 1956 and pointed out that this had been made possible by an intensive background of cultural relations.

By 1956, Peiping's cultural cold war began to prove highly effective within the territories of firm allies of the United States. Cultural exchanges with Pakistan, a military ally, for example, were climaxed in the late fall of 1956 by a state visit of the Pakistani Prime Minister to Peiping. Chinese athletes, scientists, opera troupes, etc., have been making obvious political capital in Europe and Latin America for Peiping.

Although, as indicated before, the Chinese may have overestimated the effectiveness of their cultural offensive in Japan, their gains have been substantial. They have been able to call on multiple Japanese organizations to bring pressure to bear upon Premier Kishi for the support of their foreign policy goals. It is perhaps instructive to elaborate in the case of Japan on some of the groupings used to push these goals in connection with the trade agreement breakdown in the spring of 1958.

First, of course, there is the Japan-China Friendship Association. Peiping reported on June 11, 1958 that it had instructed its branches *and affiliated organizations* to launch a great mass movement to force the Kishi Government to change its policy away from alliance with the United States toward more friendly relations with Communist China. The Association called for greater contact with trade unions and other popular organizations.[122]

Second, there are the three organizations which negotiated the fourth trade agreement in Peiping: Japanese Diet Members Union to Promote Japan-China Trade; the Japanese International Trade Promotion Association; and the Japan-China Import and Export Association of Japan. It is worth recalling that these private organizations from Japan dealt directly with central government officials in Peiping when they signed the trade agreement on March 5, 1958. The subsequent breakdown resulted from the fact that Peiping had forced them to mix up their legitimate trade interests with political issues, such as their agreement to grant the equivalent of diplomatic immunity to a Chinese Communist trade mission in Japan. Obviously in their private capacity these organizations were not empowered to make such a concession. They thus found themselves serving the foreign policy interests of the Communists when they continued to press their own government for agreement on the concessions they had made.

Third, stemming from the Japanese Socialist Party's goodwill mission to China under its head, Yoshio Suzuki, the Chinese were able to inject the China trade and recognition issue into the election campaign in Japan by having many Socialists become champions of their position against Kishi.

Fourth, there are the many isolated individuals and business firms in Japan whose livelihood can be adversely affected by any disruption of relations with the Chinese mainland. These include, for example, the steel producers whose agreement with the Chinese was cancelled in May, the Japanese fishermen, Japanese with relatives in China, newsmen and scholars who wish freer access to the mainland, and others. In the free Japanese society their individual interests can be exploited against the security of their country, without their becoming aware of it.

Fifth, in addition to the holding of trade fairs in both countries, there have been, with appropriate build-up, the exchanges of art exhibitions, athletes, etc. (even physicians!) between the Chinese mainland and Japan despite the fact that Japan does not recognize the Communist regime. Chou En-lai assured Suzuki, when he visited Peiping on December 14, 1957: "The important thing is not for the Governments to sign documents on recognition but is for the peoples to conduct interchanges with each other by all practical means."[123]

Chou and other Peiping spokesmen, of course, did not hesitate to go one step farther and point out that "the people" want exchanges and recognition, but that Kishi and his government are to blame for any difficulties. This attempt to drive a wedge between the Japanese people and their government was highly resented by many newspapers in Japan in 1958.[124] Nevertheless, Unosuke Ohta, a specialist on China affairs, writing in the June 1958 issue of the Japanese magazine *Seikai Orai* felt that the effectiveness of this Chinese campaign should not be underestimated:

> Communist China is imitating the Soviets in propaganda and other methods and activities. In recent years it has resorted to so-called "invitation diplomacy." Japanese sympathizers and progressive elements are all invited to Communist China from time to time for inspection of New China and for cultivating friendship. In view of its unusual effect, it must be regarded as marking a significant success for Red China's diplomacy.

Peiping's demands for normal trade and the establishment of normal diplomatic relations have helped the Chinese Communists promote their line that Japan is really not sovereign but under the corrupting influence of "American imperialism."

The accent upon cultural exchange also enables the Chinese Communists to sell the line that theirs is the camp of peace. All of their other activities—military, economic, and normal diplomatic—are brought within a single framework by the aid of this cultural weapon. It has thus become the most important factor in promoting a consistent and monolithic interpretation of China and Chinese intentions in Asia. China's prestige, acquiescence in Communist rule for the Chinese people, and acceptance of the doctrine of inevitability have been the results of this significant dimension of foreign relations in ever increasing sectors of Asia.

This limited discussion of the cultural cold war being waged against the West, and especially the United States, in Asia should make at least one point manifestly clear: The Communists have developed techniques which will make it highly improbable that we can conduct successful diplomacy in the same manner as we have in the past. Already developments in economic assistance and international information activities have precluded the analysis of post-World War II diplomacy in terms which might have been valid before. But it has proved difficult to work such items into an integrated foreign policy system, and thinking continues to move along conventional lines. One competent scholar, in analyzing our policy problems in Asia, for example, gives a very able presentation of advantages possessed by the United States in military, economic, and ideological instruments of foreign policy. But he finds that the military is of limited scope in Asia, the economic slow and uncertain, and that our "net score in the field of ideas is well below zero."[125] In searching for the reasons why we seem to be failing in Asia he calls attention to many of our real shortcomings and does so effectively, but the paramount importance of the Communist ability to achieve support through overt and covert organization of the natives themselves gets minor play.

The above analysis of Communist China's strategy for seizing power and Communist cultural strategy should illustrate the importance of organization. All too frequently our leaders, by failing to understand the importance of the organizational weapon, have found themselves pushed into a position of maintaining that Communist ideas have more appeal than the ideas the West has to offer. It is in terms of providing organizational backing for the presentation of our ideas and policies that our score is well below zero, not because we lack more appealing ideas and more valid approaches to the serious problems in the various countries and regions of Asia. The success of Communist propaganda in Asia, as elsewhere in the world, rests upon organization, and not wholly on content. It is organization which enables the devious Communist use of real issues like land reform, nationalism, economic development, and planning, in such a way as to hamper or prevent our own unorganized approaches from being either well thought out or effective. Perhaps the real power of the organizational weapon is illustrated by the ability of the Communist bloc to shrug off what should be the irreparable damage to their cause of such items as mass executions, slave labor, religious persecution, and countless millions of refugees—or such events as Katyn, Hungary, or Korea—or the execution of Imre Nagy. When leaders in the West begin to question the appeal and value of our ideas and some of the very foundations of our freedom, it is small wonder that Peiping and Moscow seem supremely self-confident about their new dimension of power.

CHAPTER VI

THE CONTINUING STRUGGLE

The foregoing analysis does point toward some clearly perceivable trends and conclusions regarding Communist China, its internal weaknesses and strengths, its external policies and goals, its role in changing Asia, and the implications for its relations with the non-Communist world in the years immediately ahead. Many of these conclusions are as unpleasant as they are inescapable. They cannot be evaded by cliché- and emotion-packed language or by wishful thinking.

As regards China itself, given the regime's control structure and assets discussed, there is ample reason to expect that the raw power at the disposal of the Communist leadership will continue to grow. Mao and has colleagues possess all the advantages of a totalitarian state to enable the full utilization of resources and manpower for their own goals. The interests of the Chinese people will continue to be ignored in favor of pursuit of power and doctrinal infallibility. As one observer in Hong Kong pointed out:

> The way the Communists are sacrificing human beings in colossal construction works is as contemptible as the method used by the first Emperor of the Chin Dynasty to conscript labor for the building of the Great Wall. Just as the Great Wall failed to stop the invasion from the north under which excuse the Chin Emperor justified his adventure, the industrial expansion of China today did not, nor will it in the foreseeable future, improve the livelihood of the people.[126]

To compensate for geographical problems, overpopulation, passive resistance, and the many difficulties inherent in the Chinese scene, the regime will continue to concentrate on the further development of internal state power; that is, to the point where the state monopolizes control over all remaining sectors of the society and economy. Such development can only take place by further suppression of "individualism"—that worst of all crimes in a Communist state—and with the continued terror of purges, pressures, denunciations and liquidations. David Rousset is regrettably right in concluding as to the future of the Chinese economy: "In China, as in Russia, terror must be regarded as an economic factor of great significance. Indeed it becomes a constituent element of the new productive relationships."[127] There was ample reason for, and deadly sincerity in, Liu Shao-ch'i's May 1958 promise of continued, long, hard and bitter struggle for his fellow Communists and for the Chinese people.

This is an age when knowledge is no longer measured by horizons but by solar systems. It is foolish, therefore, to gainsay the marvels which industrialization, technology, and science have already accomplished and will continue to accomplish on the Chinese mainland. Chinese people, especially the youth, are working long hours with real dedication to develop their country into a modern industrial great power. Certainly many take pride in their accomplishments and the transformation that is taking place. It is equally foolish, however, to mistake their ardor for their work and the enthusiasm accompanying the achievements of our scientific age in China as support for the regime or justification for its intellectually discredited doctrine.

Even granting it the support for scientific and industrial advance and the ability to continue the application of terror where support is not forthcoming, the Peiping regime faces serious problems in attempting to sustain its projected rate of development. Forty years of Communist failure on the land in Russia and Eastern Europe indicate that collectivized agriculture will not give the Chinese the additional production they need, a production that must cope with rising demands of 13 to 15 million additional hungry mouths each year and pay for needed imports of military and heavy industrial supplies. The peasant question is likely to prove the one on which Communist rule in China will first seriously falter and fail.

China also suffers from the weaknesses and problems of a totalitarian state. These include passive resistance, internal strains, tensions, insecurities and power rivalries. The Communists have lost much of the support and enthusiasm of the very people who helped so much to bring them to power. The revolt of the youth and the resistance of the intellectuals came into the view of the whole world in the spring of 1957. Events then indicated that the Communists had lost even more support than some of their severe external critics had claimed. Yugoslav journalists who had been in China for three years claimed in the summer of 1958 that just about every Chinese who can read and write opposes the Communist government. This is obvious exaggeration, but the general point has been sustained by the continuing "anti-Rightist" struggle, the intra-Party purges, the forced exodus of youths and intellectuals to the countryside, and almost daily reports of counterrevolutionary plots in mainland newspapers. These are an effective reminder that even the most efficiently organized terror and mass control have not eliminated man's desire for freedom. Who would be so bold as to predict success for the "people's communes" in a land where love, family, and respect for ancestors have been cherished through centuries as safeguards against overriding despotism? Developing resistance necessitates continued building of military and police power. Not unexpectedly, therefore, official statements announce plans for the further build-up and mechanization of Communist China's armed forces.

There is, in addition, the problem of bureaucracy and the corrupting influence of power. A regime which attempts to control every aspect of human action can easily become overloaded with the inefficiencies of bureaucratic wrangling and paper shuffling. This is one problem constantly recognized by Mao and his fellow members of the "new class." But their repeated purges and drives against bureaucracy indicate that they are far from solving it.

The Chinese Communist regime remains dynamic. It cannot and will not accept the status quo, either internally or abroad. It is incapable of accepting and maintaining any peace short of victory. It plans and works for continued expansion of influence and control, both in intensity and area. Mao and other top Chinese Communist leaders accept Lenin's view that "Until the final issue is decided, the state of awful war will continue."[128] They insist, along with the Soviet leaders, that the war zone must be outside the Communist bloc. As *The New York Times* pointed out in September 1958, "In line with the doctrine expounded by Mr. Khrushchev to Adlai Stevenson the Communists have a right to intervene everywhere to promote the 'wave of the future,' but the free nations have no right to intervene anywhere, not even in self-defense which becomes 'aggression' if directed against Communist expansion."[129]

When the United Nations Special Committee on Hungary issued a statement on June 21, 1958 expressing regret over the execution of Imre Nagy, Peiping denounced the action roundly: "This shameless communique is new, open interference in the internal affairs of Hungary. Who has given this disgraceful committee the right to interfere in Hungary's domestic affairs? If it is the United Nations, then who has given the UN this right? All of the various decisions on the Hungarian events reached by the United Nations are illegal and devoid of effect."[130]

With regard to the threat to world peace attending

Peiping's military thrust toward Taiwan in 1958, the *People's Daily* warned the world that this was "China's internal affair. Foreigners and the United Nations have no right to meddle in it. The Americans in Taiwan must go home. The time is not far away when the aggressors and their running dogs will all be buried."[131] This was faintly reminiscent of Khrushchev's pleasant assurance to American reporters, "We will bury you."

For their attempt to help smaller nations preserve freedom and develop economically Britain and the United States are consistently condemned by Peiping as imperialists. Premier Kishi of Japan is accused of reviving Japanese imperialism.[132] Leaders in the smaller countries who cooperate with these three powers in the attempt to maintain security and prevent subversion in the Far East are consistently denounced as "running dogs of imperialism," and oppressors of their "people." A leading Chinese Communist warned on October 11, 1958, that "as long as there is imperialism, there will be no tranquility in the world."[133] Given Peiping's ambitions and distorted approach to the world, and harking back to one of the questions raised at the outset, there is the unfortunate but unavoidable conclusion that Communist China, although an overrated power, is nevertheless a menace to world peace.

Some of the other compelling reasons for this conclusion have already been summarized. They include the economic dictates of China's plans and the problems of the Chinese scene, the inviting weakness and division as well as surplus food production of Southeast Asia, the insecurities felt by the Communist leaders because of their inability to eliminate the rival government on Taiwan, and above all the totalitarian dilemma which demands continued victories and needs external enemies in order to sustain the myths of infallibility and inevitability, channel off internal tensions, and elicit ever greater sacrifices.

A major item behind Peiping's plans and actions is the Soviet alliance. The Soviets have exploited the prestige which Communist victory in China brought, and there are many strong reasons for the Chinese leadership to continue to accept the tie as the overwhelmingly desirable short-range choice: doctrine, gearing to the Soviet economy, Russian training of technicians, dependence upon Soviet military equipment, a past record of crimes committed against fellow Chinese in the name of Soviet Communism, the necessity for not allowing the slightest puncture in the myth of infallibility, and many others. As long as Peiping's world prestige seems to be on the rise and as long as Soviet military and economic assistance help to sustain internal control, it is improbable that Mao will renounce the very force to which he has attributed his success. The alliance is further solidified by the Soviet experiences with Tito and elsewhere in Eastern Europe. These have led to a great care on the part of Moscow in handling the great ally in Asia.

Yet Peiping's problems will constitute a long-term drain on Moscow. It is unlikely that the Soviets can or will make the increasing sacrifices required to keep the alliance from being eroded by the growing demands of multiplying Chinese masses. Chinese nationalism and the growing awareness of the Chinese of their importance for Moscow are likely to make the rulers in Peiping increasingly difficult for Moscow to deal with. China has a long tradition of national pride and xenophobia and by the process of elimination there are now only the Soviet "big brothers" and the loyal Communists from Eastern Europe on whom it can focus when frustrations arise. Anti-Soviet outbursts in the spring of 1957 gave ample proof that some of these long-run forces are beginning to assert themselves and that the Chinese intellectuals especially were loath to give up traditional Chinese humanism in favor of unrelenting Leninist struggle and Marxist materialism. Privileges and expressions of power are already apparent in the lives of many of the top brass in Peiping who no longer accept former austerities. This fact adds to the demands and pressures on the Soviets.

At present the alliance itself tends to push both partners to attempt further outside gains as a part of its justification. If the advance of the Sino-Soviet bloc is halted, the internal strains and tensions and the prodigious Chinese problems will come into full play. Thus further victories are essential for Moscow and Peiping. It has frequently been argued that the firm opposition of the free world to the Moscow-Peiping axis and the economic blockade on Red China have been driving the Chinese Reds closer into the embrace of Moscow; this is probably the most effective way of breaking both the alliance and the belief in the validity of the doctrine behind it. There are real advantages in having the Soviets solely responsible for China and having the two pushed into tight embrace, especially if further victories can be prevented.

In Asia, Communist China will exploit any possibilities for further aggression by subversion and for continuing its cultural cold war. In both cases Peiping will have the advantage of its raw military power and Soviet moral and material aid for purposes of blandishment. There is, however, a possibility that the Chinese Communists will place a preponderant reliance on non-military instruments. This will be with the calculation that the organizational weapon is the most effective. But the result will not be stalemate! The struggle will not be a whit less critical for the outside world if Peiping decides to fight it with propaganda, cultural, and organizational weapons, and herein will lie major challenges for the free world in Asia.

In the face of the new Chinese power in Asia and the continuing struggle it wages, the United States, as the most powerful nation in the non-Communist world, has moved to create an alliance system and to help guarantee security of the smaller countries. Free world alliances, however, are not built like those of the Communist world on monolithic doctrine and unquestioning obedience. We have seen how Peiping has pressed hard to split allies in Asia and take advantage of the differences on policy which exist in free societies. What then are the answers to the problem of continuing struggle? What are its implications for the non-Communist nations in Asia, and especially for the United States which must bear the major share of the cost as well as the criticisms which accompany its role as the leading guarantor of security in the Far East?

1. Above all, the non-Communist world is enjoined to face up to the nature of the struggle that has been posed. It is implacable. It will continue. We must be willing to fight the cold war that has been thrust upon us with a determination to win. This cannot alone be in terms of negative and defensive anti-Communism. It requires the dedication and cooperation necessary to build viable alternatives to and refutations of Communist claims that theirs is the future.

Part of Communist China's new power in Asia has derived in reciprocal relation from the free world's passive attitude and unwillingness to assume the risks inherent in the continuing struggle—from the inability of free nations to accept it for what Communist leaders tell us it is: final and irreconcilable. Facing up to the necessity to fight the battle for freedom with the will to win is an initial first necessary step toward creating the zeal required to match Peiping's representatives in Asia.

2. Within the framework of the continuing struggle, it is necessary to combat Communist goals, to explode their prestige, to undermine their propaganda and power of attraction. The Communists in China do not possess a monopoly of industrial and scientific progress in Asia as their propagandists would like the outside world to believe. Developments in Japan and India and Taiwan are in many respects just as

remarkable, and they represent achievements without the forced labor, "people's communes," or the continued exodus of refugees by which Mao's China demonstrates that the term "free world" has solid basis in fact. We must not allow anyone to forget the crucial fact of who flees from whom.

Since every victory and every concession, however small, aids in promoting Peiping's thesis of inevitability and sowing defeatism in free areas, the non-Communist world must prevent a single further victory or any concession unmatched by Communist concession accompanied by built-in enforceable guarantees. Under no conditions must the free nations in Asia be persuaded or allowed to give in to Chinese Communist force or blandishment. As former President Harry S. Truman said in supporting the United States stand during the Quemoy crisis in September 1958: "Whenever and wherever we are challenged by the Communists in their constant probing for weak spots in our determination to protect our freedom and the peace, we must meet that challenge resolutely, swiftly, and as a united people."[134]

3. In addition to keeping its powder dry, the free world must develop some of the very organizational weapons used by Communism in order to cancel out its advantages, especially in the economically underdeveloped areas around China. This does not mean the abandonment of free institutions. What is meant here is the building of organizations composed of national groupings to support free world alliances and policies with cultural, economic, scientific, and educational programs. Mao and his colleagues have proclaimed that the Chinese pattern of "liberation" is to be applied in Asia, Africa, and Latin America. Unless the free world can develop organizational competition for the Communist organizational weapon in these areas, it is probable that no amount of economic or military assistance nor even the best of propaganda can prevent further Communist successes.

It is upon organizations of nationals of the various countries around China that we must rely for the exposure of the human realities behind the seeming successes and appeals of the Mao regime. Communism has destroyed national traditions as well as whole nations within the areas it controls; it should be suffering setbacks in attempts to appeal to nationalism in Asia. Obviously Chinese Communist cultural diplomacy and appreciation of organizational power have more than overcome such drawbacks.

A good example of where the United States and some of the other Western powers have fallen down in the past is in the failure to provide national organizations and *esprit de corps* for the many foreign students from underdeveloped lands. Perhaps one of the main reasons that thousands of Chinese trained in the United States are now arrayed against America is that they were never provided with an organization with American support and dedicated to the cause of democracy in their country. Each went back to China as an individual. It would be a matter of relatively small effort and expense for the United States and its Western allies to provide the framework which will enable foreign students to return to their countries with a sense of mission and a feeling of belonging to a group and a movement for achieving that mission. Each national grouping of foreign students could be given the support to convince them that the United States, the free world, and their own people are counting on them for the future industrialization, improved standards of living, and cultural development of their nation. This is but one small example of the type of activity which the free world must develop in a field where we have hardly begun to operate and where we actually have many advantages over the Communist bloc.

We dare not overlook the national pride, the enthusiasm of youth (who predominate in most countries in Asia), and the general feeling of "wanting to belong" which exist in many of the countries immediately threatened by Communist China. Responses to the first attempts by the Southeast Asia Treaty Organization in the fields of cultural and scientific exchange and the creation of auxiliary organizations have already indicated the tremendous potential support for the free world existing in that area. Unless the free world is ready to provide structure and organization for this support, it has small hope of preventing further Communist victories.

4. Another implication of Communist China's continuing struggle is that the free world must exploit every asset it possesses. One of these is the continued existence on Taiwan of the Republic of China which possesses all the advantages of a government-in-exile in time of war. There has been an unfortunate lack of information in many areas of the free world on the real accomplishments of ten million Chinese in Taiwan. Concentration on military problems has frequently prevented a realization of the extent to which Taiwan has become a viable symbol and repository of Chinese national culture. Following a visit there in December 1956, for example, Brian Crozier of the foreign staff of the London *Economist* observed: "The British public is ill-informed about Formosa, and indeed about the Chinese question in general . . . it is as though a shutter was drawn across people's minds in 1950, when the British government decided to recognize Mao Tse-tung's Communist regime." In a pamphlet entitled "I Was Wrong about Free China," Crozier went on to say:

> In retrospect, I number myself among the ignorant majority. As a result of my visit to Formosa at the end of last year, I have revised the views I held about the Nationalist government as an instrument for combatting communism in Asia, and about the American policy of supporting that government. I am now certain that the Nationalist government deserves the support of all who oppose communism, and that the policy of the United States in aiding the Republic of China is the correct one. Any other

policy can only lead to another bloodless victory for communism.[135]

Professor E. Stuart Kirby of the University of Hong Kong visited Taiwan in April 1955. He too had supported the British position on China in 1951, but following his stay in the Republic of China he wrote:

> There is firm ground in Taiwan, despite many difficulties and the impossibility of seeing very exactly into the future. It is not a question of obstinate resistance to the further advance of Communism, but of building up, and demonstrating in practice, a positive alternative to it in Chinese, Asian and international terms. This is well realized, and is being more boldly attempted than is generally appreciated abroad.

The next year, following a trip to the Communist mainland, Professor Kirby, after noting the "drabness and lack of color or 'sparkle' in the people, in their living conditions, their dress, their demeanor, in everything," concluded that the Republic of China represented "more of the real China than was to be found in the Russianized mainland system."[136]

It has been argued that the United States support of Taiwan and refusal to recognize the Peiping government is regarded by leaders in Asia as an insult to Asian nationalism (if such a thing exists). This is probably more of an indication of the effectiveness of Communist cold war effort than a measure of the validity of United States policy. As a leader of the free world, the United States must be willing to run risks. Continued steadfastness and unwavering support of smaller allies are far more valuable long-range contributions to free world security than momentary popularity gained through concessions.

Willingness to face the continuing struggle with a determination to win, and especially in Asia where the stakes are so large, should help the free world to tap its own vast economic potential, one of its greatest advantages over the Communist bloc. This will require an increasing awareness of the needs and varied nationalistic demands of peoples in Asia, and for some areas it calls for effective long-range planning. But economic assistance will be of limited value unless it can be carried on in terms which relate organized groups from the country to be aided to free world willingness to support them and their aspirations for their own country. Here, again, there has been a communications breakdown in the free world with respect to Taiwan and the remarkable record of the Chinese-American Joint Commission on Rural Reconstruction. Various foreign observers and United Nations officials have hailed this organization as probably the most successful example of the administration of foreign aid in the world. A truly significant aspect of the work of this commission is that it has been helping to provide local organizations (4-H clubs, etc.) which have made democracy come alive in local areas in Taiwan.

5. Also implicit in what has been said above is the necessity for the free world to develop its own new dimensions of political warfare in the continuing struggle. We must be willing to exploit the weaknesses of the enemy, to make him fail. Through scholarships, lectureships, and ceremonies, for example, local organizations backing free world alliances can help keep alive the names of those who have been persecuted or have paid the ultimate price under Communism in order that their people can be constantly reminded of the real nature of the Communist system.

In their 1848 *Communist Manifesto* Marx and Engels claimed that the bourgeoisie had forged the weapons of their own destruction. More than a century later it is obvious that Communism has forged the weapons for its own destruction and that freedom is the specter that is haunting the Communist world. In China the armed communes can prove the downfall of Mao's regime. Recantation and execution provide a constant reminder to the people that the totalitarian system cannot trust them. Struggle against the outside world tells them they have allies.

Communist states are highly centralized bureaucracies. They respond to stimuli from the outside; they can be forced by challenge and competition to enter into unintended fields of activity where they are at a disadvantage; they are vulnerable to organizational disruption. But the free world has put little sustained or systematic drive into such efforts. In World War II the allies marshalled the greatest scientists and gave them unlimited funds to develop atomic weapons for hot war. Can we not do the same thing to engage in the continuing struggle on the political and organizational level—a struggle which is just as deadly? Unless the free world develops its capacities for struggle on the political plane Peiping and Moscow will continue to make a war zone of the non-Communist world.

6. One final item is implicit in the Chinese Communist challenge and the continuing struggle: the necessity to recognize that the conflict is global. This makes the provincialism of the West, or of any area, not only foolish but dangerous. Both Communist China and the Soviet Union are placing heavy emphasis on foreign area training as well as science. The West especially has retained a complacent and smug concentration on the self-study of its own civilization. While we have every reason to be proud of the vitality, exuberance and wonder of our own civilization, we must recognize that others have a right to be proud of theirs too. Victory for the free world may well depend on building the cultural appreciation and exchange which will convince all nations that their pride, their values, and their opportunity for self-respect can only be realized in an association which can organize a peace zone of the whole free world in the continuing struggle.

NOTES

1. For example, Chester Bowles in his *Ambassador's Report* (New York, Harper, 1953) laments our ignorance of Asia but himself generalizes on the "existence of an Asian viewpoint, held by half of all the people in the world, from Japan to the Mediterranean." (p. 387) This type of generalization, reflective of Bowles' Indian experience and contacts with some Indian leaders who have presumed to speak for Asia, unfortunately detracts from the value of some of his other very prescient comments about events, issues, and personalities in India. This willingness to generalize about Asia in terms of its people (it is, after all, only a geographical expression) also permeates the writings of Justice William O. Douglass. The approach obscures national and cultural differences and prevents the presentation of local issues such as land tenure in the distinct manner in which they must be treated for effective handling. Even more, it frequently leads unwittingly to acceptance of Communist-inspired interpretation of local problems in terms of Asia-wide "feudalism" and suppression by imperialism, enabling and aiding local acceptance of the two-camp view of the world discussed later in the text. (Feudalism, a distinctive Western political institution has, with the possible exception of Japan, never existed in most of Asia anyway.)

2. Translations from the *People's Daily* are distributed on a daily basis by the New China News Agency, but these are for external consumption and frequently edit out items which the Chinese are anxious only for the people at home to have. The serial publications of the American Consulate General in Hong Kong (available in most large libraries in the United States and in centers abroad) frequently produce full translations from this official paper as well as from other publications. In preparing this survey I have attempted to limit references to further materials on particular aspects of such English-language sources. There is ample documentation available in English for the points made here.

3. Harry Paxton Howard, *America's Role in Asia*, New York, Howell, Soskin, 1943, p. 28.

4. Kuo Ping-chia, *China, New Age and New Outlook*, New York, Knopf, 1956, p. 207. It should be noted that this latter conclusion is based upon the explicit assumption that "On the whole, one nation functions pretty much like another, whether it is communistic or capitalistic." (p. 218)

5. On two Department of State studies of Communist bloc aid to and penetration of underdeveloped lands with summary texts, see *The New York Times* of January 5 and January 15, 1958. The Council for Economic and Industry Research, Inc. study of "Foreign Assistance Activities of the Communist Bloc and their Implications for the United States," is published as pp. 619-766 of Senate Document No. 52, *Foreign Aid Program*, 85th Congress, 1st Session.

6. For a good analysis of problems involved in dealing with mainland statistics, see *China News Analysis* (hereafter *CNA*), weekly newsletter, P.O. Box 5517, Kowloon, Hong Kong, No. 196, September 13, 1957, pp. 1-7. This weekly edited by the Jesuit Father LaDany is a reliable and very valuable source for following mainland developments.

7. Official figures on the number of collectives have been vague. According to Minister of Agriculture Liao Yu-yen's report of February 1, 1958 there were 780,000 collectives as of June 1957. With the new and larger "communes" being formed in place of the collectives the number will be smaller, but the problem of gathering accurate statistical data remains unchanged.

8. David Rousset, "The Crisis in the Economic Structures of People's China," *Far Eastern Economic Review* (hereafter *FEER*), September 12, 1957, pp. 326-331.

9. *CNA*, No. 182, May 24, 1957, p. 5.

10. Unfortunately outside analysts of the Chinese Communist economy, in attempting to make an appraisal, are frequently in a position of having to use and reproduce statistics many of which Peiping itself admits are unreliable and others which have an obviously propagandistic genesis. Solomon Adler's *The Chinese Economy* (New York, Monthly Review Press, 1957) is wholly uncritical and laudatory and in most respects doubles for an official publication from Peiping for foreign consumption. Alexander Eckstein in his economic chapter of *Moscow-Peking Axis* (New York, Harper, 1957) raises few cautions. Ygael Gluckstein, *Mao's China* (Boston, Beacon, 1957) questions some figures and uses local self-criticism to discredit others, but relies on official statistics for his projections because of the lack of alternative figures at the national level. The most recent United Nations ECAFE study "Industrialization in a Centrally Planned Economy (Mainland China)," *Economic Survey of Asia and the Far East 1957*, Bangkok, March 1958, pp. 86-111, notes the "significant gaps in data," and points out that "in

many instances it is possible that no reliable statistics exist." Although I, too, am faced with the problem of having to use Peiping's statistics, I do want to go on record as having some grave reservations, especially about those statistics dealing with the agrarian scene. For example, many of the claims for 1958, the year of the "great leap forward," such as Liu Shao-ch'i's statement to the Party Congress on May 5, 1958 that irrigated land had increased by 58,195,098 acres between September 30, 1957 and April 30, 1958, are obviously absurd. That he should claim to have such figures by May 5 is already an indication of their patently ridiculous nature.

11. Quoted in Ricardo (pseud.), "China Realities," *FEER*, December 8, 1957, pp. 713-716.

12. A good example of an account of China's industrial progress and other developments by an independent observer is the series of articles by Walton A. Cole, editor of *Reuters,* who visited the mainland. His articles were published in *The New York Times* from February 24 through February 27, 1958. In some cases Peiping's propaganda for the outside world gives pictures which confirm some of the claimed industrial developments. The *Peking Review* of July 8, 1958, for example, contains pictures of China's first atomic reactor. The *Peking Review* is an English language weekly published by the Communists in Peiping.

13. That such late statistics are available in a land where national statistical work is admittedly still in its infancy can be regarded as an indication of the extent of centralized control, but, as indicated in note 10, it throws doubt on the statistics themselves. For two examples of pictorial accounts of China's industrial growth which would tend to support the figures in the table, see John W. Davenport, "China Passes a Dividend," *Fortune,* September 1957, pp. 151ff. and "Red China on the March," *Life,* January 21, 1957, pp. 107-115. Peiping produces two monthly pictorials with English text: *China Pictorial* and *China Reconstructs.*

14. See the dispatch of A. M. Rosenthal from Vienna, dated October 20, 1958.

15. This resolution is reproduced in the *Peking Review* of September 16, 1958, pp. 21-23. For a good collection of early Communist documents dealing with the communes see the 75-page issue of the *Current Background* series issued by the American Consulate General in Hong Kong, entitled "People's Communes in Communist China," No. 517, September 5, 1958. The August 29, 1958 issue of the *Union Research Service* (hereafter *URS*), "A Big, Bold Step Towards Communism," explains how the communes have fused the functions of formerly separated cooperatives such as the credit co-ops, the supply and marketing co-ops, the agricultural producers' cooperatives, and others in the countryside. *URS,* issued twice a week by the Union News

Agency, 110 Waterloo Road, Kowloon, Hong Kong, frequently trans-
lates materials from local mainland newspapers which are smuggled
out to Hong Kong because they are not permitted to circulate either
outside or between provinces. This makes the service especially valuable for following local developments on the mainland. For later documents dealing with the development of people's communes see the
Hong Kong Consulate General's *Survey of China Mainland Press* series
(hereafter *SCMP*), No. 1860, September 24, 1958, pp. 5-45. A brief survey of the communes in the *FEER,* September 25, 1958, pp. 394-395, is
entitled "Peking's Control over the Rural Population." Its conclusion:
"In reality, Peking persists in its practice of 'from each the maximum
amount of work and sacrifice and to each the minimum ration of food
and other necessities.' The formation of people's communes, therefore,
serves only one purpose—it enables Peking to tighten its control over
the rural population." The able reporting of Tillman Durdin of *The
New York Times* from Hong Kong and the analysis of Harry Schwartz
in the same newspaper have given good coverage of the people's commune movement in China.

16. *CNA,* No. 246, September 26, 1958. This very able survey
gives historical background analysis of the model regulation published
in the *People's Daily* of September 4, 1958, as well as a discussion of
the full implications of the common kitchen. Probably only one who
has experienced the losses of individual freedom involved in barracks
life in the armed services or who has suffered in a concentration camp
or prison can fully appreciate the fate of the Chinese peasants in the
communes.

17. These figures are quoted from an *NCNA* dispatch in *The
New York Times* of October 12, 1958.

18. On this drive during the summer of 1958 to take over private homes see *URS* for July 29, 1958 entitled "Socialist Transformation
of Private House Ownership Gains Momentum."

19. Li Wen-shan, " 'Field Platoon' Plays Important Role,"
People's Daily, August 15, 1958; *Current Background,* No. 517, pp. 58-60.

20. As *CNA,* No. 246 points out, "This is a startling measure,
since 'labour reform', or 'labour in the collectives under surveillance'
is an officially admitted form of criminal sanction, but no official document had previously said that local administrative organizations may
impose this kind of forced labour." (p. 4)

21. Quoted by Harry Schwartz, *The New York Times,* September 7, 1958.

22. Such accounts are frequently carried as feature stories by
newspapers in the outside world, but they have become so commonplace
that they do not seem to get the attention they merit. See, for example,
two stories in *The New York Times* of May 23, and May 24, 1958 dealing with refugees in Macao.

23. For a critical account of slave labor in Communist China see K. A. Wittfogel, "Forced Labor in Communist China," *Problems of Communism*, 5.4, July-August 1956, pp. 34-42. See also Peter S. H. Tang, *Communist China Today* (New York, Praeger, 1957), pp. 238-250 and Gluckstein, *Mao's China*, pp. 287-292. An interesting Communist defense of the mainland's system of forced labor can be found in the *Extracts from China Mainland Magazines* (hereafter *ECMM*), No. 140, August 25, 1958, pp. 6-11. *ECMM* contains translations of important articles from leading Communist magazines and is issued weekly by the American Consulate General in Hong Kong. The article in question by Li Shao-sheng is entitled "Refutation of the Slander of the Rightists Against the Policy of Reform Through Labor for Criminals," and is translated from the Communist *Political and Legal Studies* magazine of June 20, 1958.

24. On forced migrations see *URS*, February 22, 1957, "Vast Population Movement to Communist China's Wastelands"; and the issues of October 15, 1957; January 3, 1958; and May 23, 1958. A useful summary of forced migrations and the "opening up of virgin lands" is given in CNA No. 212, January 17, 1958, pp. 1-7. See FEER, June 5, 1958, "Chinese Students off to the Countryside," pp. 713-715.

25. Various issues of *URS* have translated provincial newspapers telling of local revolts. See, for example, the issues of November 12 and December 27, 1957, and those of January 14 and 24, March 4, April 18, and July 8, 1958.

26. A somewhat skeptical account of developments in transport in China is contained in *CNA*, No. 213, January 24, 1958, pp. 1-7. For a glowing account with a map showing Communist construction of and plans for railroads and highways, see *China Pictorial*, July, 1958, pp. 19-21.

27. An institutional and historical assessment of this factor and its relation to military power and centralized despotism is given in Karl A. Wittfogel's *Oriental Despotism* (New Haven, Yale, 1957), pp. 50-66.

28. For a full translation of an article dealing with the Ming Tombs Reservoir project see *URS*, June 20, 1958. The *URS* editor remarks in an introduction to the document that this is just a "part of the never-ending process of making everyone completely submissive to the Communist Party leadership." The August issue of *China Reconstructs* contains an illustrated article on the project, "Socialist Labour Builds a Dam," by Tan Ai-chiang. The issue of *China Pictorial* for the same month, p. 18, shows the ambassador to China from the United Arab Republic joining in the work.

29. Summarized from a *Pravda* article by Harry Schwartz, *The New York Times*, October 12, 1958.

30. Quoted in CNA No. 179, May 3, 1957, p. 5.

31. For an analysis of Sino-Soviet trade, see *URS*, September 2, 1958 and its "Supplement."

32. The 1957 ration was 16 Chinese feet per person. See *The New York Times* of August 20 and 22, 1957 and its Editorial of August 29. The *Survey of China Mainland Press* of the American Consulate General, Hong Kong, No. 1600, August 28, 1957, pp. 1-10, contains official dispatches on the cotton crisis of 1957. See also *CNA*, No. 180, May 10, 1957, pp. 2-7; No. 188, July 12, 1957, pp. 1-7; No. 209, December 13, 1957, p. 5; and No. 224, April 18, 1958, p. 6.

33. Article by Lu Teh-jun in *Wen Hui Pao*, Shanghai, March 5, 1957. Lu's projection of China's population: 810 million in 10 years, 930 million in 15 years.

34. Actually, preparation for the introduction of state-sponsored dissemination of birth control knowledge began in August 1953 when the Cabinet gave instructions that the Ministry of Public Health should assist the public in birth control. The first reported open discussion, however, did not come until September of the following year when Shao Li-tzu raised the subject at the National People's Congress. The Communists seldom mentioned birth control in connection with a population problem; it was usually presented as a method for preserving the health of mothers. Obviously the greatest resistance was in the countryside. As the supplement to the *Wen Hui Pao* of January 22, 1957 pointed out, "In many regions not even the public-health officials dare speak openly of birth control. Propaganda is abundant in the cities; it has not yet penetrated to the villages." See *CNA*, No. 172, March 15, 1957.

35. *SCMP*, No. 1647, pp. 6-7.

36. The editorial from the *Wen-Hui Pao* and a related article from the same newspaper are translated in *SCMP*, No. 1845, pp. 17-20. The article attacking the views of Ma Yin-ch'u is translated in *ECMM*, No. 142, September 15, 1958, pp. 25-32. For a study of Peiping's party line switches on birth control and poulation problems see the article by E. S. Kirby, "Peiping's Growing Dilemma—Population," *Problems of Communism*, 7.2, March-April 1958. On the more recent reversion to Marxist orthodoxy and the dispute over the entrance of the venerable Chinese scholar Ma Yin-ch'u into the argument see also *URS*, May 2, May 6, and May 20, 1958. For another statement of the 1958 official position see Su Chung, "Facts About China's Population," *Peking Review*, July 1, 1958, pp. 9-10. This makes an interesting contrast with the views expressed by various leaders at the 1957 Session of the Chinese People's Political Consultative Conference National Committee. These latter are reproduced in *Current Background*, No. 445. A well-documented study by Shih Ch'eng-chih (pseud.) of the difficulties and delusions which have beset the Chinese Communists in dealing with the problems of population appeared in three parts in the Chinese language

Hong Kong journal, *China Weekly (Tsu-kuo),* June 16, 23, and 30, 1958; this series of articles deserves translation.

37. United Nations, ECAFE, *Economic Bulletin for Asia and the Far East,* 8.4, Bangkok, March 1958, p. 111.

38. For an excellent summary of the population problem on the world scale see Karl Sax, "The Population Explosion," Foreign Policy Association, *Headline Series,* No. 120, Nov.-Dec. 1956.

39. ECAFE, *Economic Bulletin for Asia and the Far East,* 7.3, Bangkok, November 1956, p. 32.

40. Of course collectives and communes offer a centralized state more initial tax take, but in terms of long-range approach, experience in the Soviet Union and Eastern Europe (amply documented) argues that failure to understand the farmer and appreciate human nature offers dismal prospects for the Communist program. There are indications from the Chinese Communist press that the same forces which have spelled failure for the Communists elsewhere in the world are taking their toll in China. See, for example, the July 2, 1957 issue of *URS* entitled "Contradictions Between the Peasantry and the Communist Party," that of October 1, 1957 entitled "Rural Resentment in Kwangtung," that of October 29, 1957, "Peasants Continue to Hoard Grain," that of May 17, 1957, "Collectives Let Draft Animals Die in Large Numbers," and that of November 26, 1957, "Austerity Measures Tightened; Further Cuts in Grain Ration." All of these issues contain translations from mainland newspapers. On the relationship between the collectives and the food problem see also *CNA,* No. 189, July 19, 1957; No. 204, November 8, 1957, and No. 222, March 28, 1958. China's population problem is serious enough, but Peiping's determination to move ahead with heavy industrialization at the expense of the peasants only threatens further aggravation and stands in marked contrast with the methods being employed to cope with the food problem created by the population explosion elsewhere in the world. For a good summary of other problems faced in Peiping's approach to the peasant family see Peggy Durdin, "Deep Challenge to China's Communists," *The New York Times Magazine,* June 15, 1958.

41. *CNA,* No. 190, July 26, 1957, p. 2. For U.S. figures see Department of Commerce, *Statistical Abstracts of the United States 1957,* p. 616.

42. Few books have done as good a job of presenting the agrarian problem of China as has Gerald F. Winfield, *China, the Land and the People,* New York, Sloane, 1948. See also Gluckstein, pp. 19-24 and 79-97.

43. In Taiwan where there were only about 875,000 hectares of land cultivated compared with 112,660,000 hectares on the mainland, over 550,000 tons of chemical fertilizers were applied to the land in 1957. In order to match this Peiping would have to apply more than 70 million tons of chemical fertilizers or more than the total world production!

Nevertheless in 1958 Peiping began to claim phenomenal success in increasing agricultural production. The claim in the July 8, 1958, issue of the *Peking Review* (p. 3) that "This year's summer food crops, however, are almost 60 per cent higher than that of last year . . ." would seem to be one of those claims which throw great doubt on the reliability of Chinese Communist statistics.

44. On petroleum problems see *CNA*, No. 220, March 14, 1958, pp. 1-7.

45. For one of the *NCNA* dispatches on the Szechuan "discoveries" see *SCMP*, No. 1844, September 2, 1958, p. 20. The quotation and statistics are from the article by Chien Feng, "Petroleum in Central Szechuan," *China Pictorial*, October, 1958, pp. 8-11.

46. Peiping Radio, Home Service, October 19, 1958.

47. For a good example of Communist claims of great resources see "China's Mineral Wealth," in the *Peking Review* of May 10, 1958.

48. Peiping Radio, Home Service, September 29, 1958; *The New York Times*, October 23, 1958.

49. For discussion of Soviet nationalities problems with bibliographic notes see Frederick C. Barghoorn, *Soviet Russian Nationalism*, New York, Oxford, 1956. Basic material on China's minorities and early Communist policies can be found in Peter S. H. Tang, *Communist China Today*, New York Praeger, 1957, pp. 200-217.

50. The unreliability of these figures is pointed out in *CNA*, No. 232, June 13, 1958. This whole issue of *CNA* is devoted to the National Minority Problem and the development of resistance during the first half of 1958. An indication of how frequently sources in the West accept such Communist claims as, for example, this figure on the area occupied by the minority nationalities is its use in *The New York Times* editorial of January 19, 1958 which is otherwise soundly critical of Peiping's policies.

51. For a discussion of the establishment of the Kwangsi Autonomous Area and documents connected with it see *Current Background*, No. 504, April 15, 1958. See also *CNA*, No. 192, August 9, 1957.

52. This speech with commentary by Geoffrey F. Hudson, an outstanding British scholar and authority on Communist China, was published as a special section of *The New Leader*, September 9, 1957. For Mao's discussion of the national minorities question see pp. 42-43.

53. Peiping's problems in Tibet have been fairly well covered in the outside press. For detailed treatment of more recent developments as well as translations of important documents and local newspapers containing self-criticism and information not to be found elsewhere see *Current Background*, No. 409, September 21, 1956, "Conditions in Tibet and Tibetan Autonomous Areas," and also No. 490, February 7, 1958 and No. 505, May 1, 1958 both entitled "Recent Reports on Tibet," and *URS*, November 12, 1957, "Regional Autonomy for Tibetans in

Yunnan," December 27, 1957, "Tibetans and Other Minorities Still Giving Trouble; Peiping's Attitude Hardens," and January 14, 1958, "Role of Monks in Tibet." See also *FEER,* August 8, 1957, "Tibet and Great Han Chauvinism," pp. 171 ff.

54. Vice-Premier Ho Lung in his address to the First People's Congress of the Kwangsi Chuang Autonomous Region, *Current Background,* No. 504, p. 6.

55. See *URS,* March 19, 1957, "Racial Problems in Remote Sinkiang," and July 8, 1958, "Local Nationalism Persists in Sinkiang." See also the column by Harry Schwartz in *The New York Times* of July 5, 1958.

56. The full account of the 55-day session of the Tsinghai CCP Provincial Committee which expelled Governor Sun Tso-pin was published in the Tsinghai *Daily* of Sining on March 11, 1958. The translation from this difficult to procure provincial newspaper constitutes the whole issue of *URS,* April 18, 1958.

57. On the Moslems in China and developments in early 1958 see *CNA,* No. 226, May 2, 1958, pp. 1-7.

58. On the movement of the Hui people out of Honan, see *CNA,* No. 226, p. 6; and No. 212, January 17, 1958, p. 3. The *People's Daily* carried an account by a correspondent on January 10, 1957, of life among over 40,000 Moslems, including 17-year old girls who had been moved from Honan to Sinkiang. He reported that since no houses had been built, they lived in caves and that many of them found the "labor discipline hard."

59. On the revolt in Honan, see *The New York Times,* May 18, 1958. The New China News Agency carried a dispatch on August 18, 1957 describing the denunciation and confession of the Vice-Chairman of the Chinese Moslem People's Cultural Association; this was during the period when a great many Moslem weeds appeared in Mao's flower garden.

60. In addition to the sources quoted above on minority problems, see also *Current Background,* No. 500, March 31, 1958 which contains statements on minorities problems at the 5th session of the 1st National Peoples Congress in Peiping, and *URS,* January 24, 1958, March 4, 1958 and September 5, 1958; also *SCMP,* No. 1839, August 25, 1958.

61. On Peiping's program of economic aid to other regions see *FEER,* May 8, 1958, p. 580.

62. Actually the percentage of the national budget given to military build-up is much higher, but the Chinese Communists follow the Soviet policy of hiding many military appropriations under such headings as Ministry of Heavy Industry, etc.

63. On the effects of the Western embargo on oil and oil-drilling equipment see the dispatch from London by Drew Middleton in *The*

New York Times of January 30, 1958. This article also discusses some Sino-Soviet tensions over advice from the "big brothers" and over production methods.

64. Talk about the impressive achievements made by Peiping in the heavy industry field and about Sino-Soviet tensions has even gone to the extreme of speculation that the Kremlin is afraid that Soviet power will be eclipsed by China. It is doubtful whether the Soviets are bothered about this possibility arising even in the twenty-first century. They are probably much more concerned about the possibility of having to pour ever greater aid down the manhole of endless Chinese humanity.

65. Mao and his colleagues at the top of the Chinese Communist hierarchy are first and always military men. See my article "The Chinese Red Army," in the *New Republic,* May 13, 1957, pp. 39-42.

66. For examples of the Chinese use of division within the United States and problems between the United States and its allies over the Quemoy crisis in August and September 1958, see the issues of the *Peking Review* and such articles as that by Tsui Chi "Cornered!" in the issue of October 7, 1958, pp. 11-12.

67. A description of the October 1, 1958 parade in Peiping is contained in a special article in the *Peking Review,* October 7, 1958, pp. 6-8, entitled "A Nation Rejoices."

68. There are now many good studies of monolithic controls inside Communist China and of the dull, drab uniformity which has settled upon the people as a result. An early study which called outside attention to the psychological implications of control in China was Edward Hunter, *Brain-Washing in Red China,* New York, Vanguard, 1951. It is still a valid description and makes chilling reading. For a more recent account of conformity in China see Robert Guillain, *600 Million Chinese,* New York, Criterion, 1957 and the article by Richard Hughes, "Are There Seeds of Revolt in Red China?" *The New York Times Magazine,* November 2, 1958.

69. We should not underestimate the impression made upon the Chinese as well as their leaders by the industrial advances under Communism. In a country which has been almost exclusively agrarian the presence of machine tools of home manufacture, of Chinese-made trucks and buses, and of heavy electrical equipment, to mention but a few items, can easily give the impression that the regime does possess almost magical power after all.

70. Western analysts frequently fail to appreciate the extent to which Lenin's strategic division of the world into the "camp of imperialism" versus the "camp of socialism" has provided the framework within which current events are interpreted by Peiping and a basis for unwavering support for Soviet primacy on the part of Mao.

71. The March 1958 issue of the ECAFE *Bulletin* gives a useful survey of the varying role of planning in economic development in Asia.

72. There has been some academic disagreement about the role of Mao and much talk about "Maoism." A close reading of the works of Mao and of international Communist documents does not sustain this. Unfortunately, some students of Chinese Communism in the United States in order to justify their Maoist thesis have even gone to the extreme of excising from documents they have reproduced statements where Mao gives credit to Stalin and Moscow and insists on Soviet primacy. One documentary study of Chinese Communism published in the United States and abroad fails to treat the Chinese Communist reaction to the Hitler-Stalin Pact, the Soviet-Japanese Neutrality Treaty, or the Soviet looting of Manchurian industry after World War II. On these and other items not handled Mao's immediate and consistent support for Stalin indicated his overriding commitment to Moscow-led Communism at the expense of China's national interest. (See, *A Documentary History of Chinese Communism* by Brandt, Fairbank, and Schwartz; Harvard, Cambridge, 1952). The determination to maintain that Chinese Communism is somehow different has led to some interesting switches on the part of some observers of the Chinese scene. The very same people who, following Mao's speech on letting the hundred flowers bloom, maintained that Mao was liberalizing the Communist movement, were one year later maintaining that Mao is an arch-Stalinist and therefore out of tune with liberalizing tendencies in the Soviet Union. For a convincing presentation of the thesis of Mao's subservience to Moscow see Peter S. H. Tang, *Communist China Today.*

73. Herbert Ritvo, "Moscow, Peiping and the Middle East," *Problems of Communism.* 7.5, Sept.-Oct. 1958, pp. 47-49.

74. The text of Chou's address is printed in the *Peking Review,* October 7, 1958, pp. 10-11.

75. Key documents of the Second Session of the Eighth National Congress of the CCP were published in a special enlarged issue of the *Peking Review,* No. 14, June 3, 1958.

76. From *China Today,* published by the American Friends of the Chinese People, New York, January 1934.

77. Peiping Radio, July 18, 1958. The return to an aggressive Anti-United States policy was evident in the internal Chinese press (though not to the outside world) shortly after Mao's return from the anniversary celebrations in Moscow in 1957. By the spring of 1958 it was apparent that Peiping, in a manner similar to that of 1950, was laying a solid propaganda basis for possible hostilities with the United States. During much of 1956 and 1957 the "paper tiger" line had all but disappeared.

78. In addition to the Treatment of Moscow-Peiping relations in Peter Tang's *Communist China Today,* see Chapter 11 of my *China Under Communism* (New Haven, Yale, 1955). The Council on Foreign Relations Volume by H. L. Boorman and others, *Moscow-Peking Axis*

(New York, Harper, 1957) examines some of the strains and possible sources of conflict. A more recent item in *URS* of December 10, 1957 entitled "Learn Soviet Experience—With Qualifications." See *CNA*, No. 179, May 3, 1957; No. 205, November 15, 1957 which discusses resentment against Russian experts; and No. 223, April 11, 1958 which discusses the Russian impact on Chinese culture. *FEER*, May 29, 1958, "Maoism and International Communism," pp. 676-677.

79. In addition to the source mentioned in note 76, documents on the Party Congress are published as issues 507 and 508 of the *Current Background* series.

80. Chou En-lai's speech to the Congress delivered September 16, 1956 is reproduced in *Current Background*, No. 413. For those who entertain any doubts about China's overriding commitment to the two-camp view of the world and the extent to which all aspects of life in China are subordinated to the great Marxist world struggle, the reading of the documents of the 8th Party Congress will prove informative. These are published in three volumes in Peiping and are also reproduced in the *Current Background* series, Nos. 410 through 427.

81. See *The New York Times*, July 2, 1957. On economic difficulties encountered in 1957, see *CNA*, No. 189, pp. 1-7, and the article in *FEER*, cited in Note 8.

82. *People's Daily*, December 25, 1952.

83. Interestingly enough, the Tokyo *Shimbun* reprinted this quotation for its readers on June 11, 1958, in an article entitled "Why is Red China Adopting a Stiff Attitude."

84. *Current Background*, No. 342.

85. *Survey of China Mainland Press*, No. 1686.

86. For documents and analysis of the events discussed in this paragraph see *URS* of September 19 and September 23, 1958, "Communist Menace to Hong Kong," Parts I and II. *NCNA* dispatches and translations from mainland newspapers dealing with the campaign against the British are to be found in *SCMP*, Nos. 1843-1847, August 29-September 5, 1958.

87. *NCNA*, Peiping, February 23, 1958.

88. *People's Daily*, Peiping, March 5 and 6, 1958.

89. These events are covered in *The New York Times* of March and April 1958.

90. The timing and facts in the Nagasaki case were reviewed by Yoshio Nakano, "Deterioration of Japan-Communist China Relations and the Press," in the Japanese Monthly, *Seakai*, for July 1958.

91. *The New York Times*, May 8, 1958.

92. *SCMP*, No. 1772, May 15, 1958, p. 42 and *Peking Review*, May 13, 1958, p. 17.

93. See *The New York Times* editorial analysis of the Japanese elections on May 24, 1958.

94. *NCNA*, Peiping, June 4, 1958.

95. *NCNA*, Peiping, June 11, 1958.

96. The Japanese newspaper *Asahi*, for example, in a survey on the advance of Communist China's merchandise into Southeast Asia on September 7, estimated mainland China's trade with that area at $520 million or 20 per cent higher than in 1957.

97. Tadao Nishimura, Assistant Foreign News Editor of the *Yomiuri* reported this in that newspaper on July 7, 1958. He noted that the Chinese who are famed for their hospitality would never have treated Japanese reporters in such a cold manner by sheer accident and added, "I warn the Japanese Government as well as the Japanese people not to take an optimistic view on the present stiff attitude of Communist China.

98. These conditions were printed in an article in the October issue of *Chuo Koron* by Sata. Sata is the former head of the international bureau of the Japanese Socialist Party.

99. This was the opening sentence of an article "On the Sata Report and Attitude of Red China," by Naka Funada, Chairman of the Liberal-Democratic Party Foreign Affairs Research Council, published in *Mainichi*, September 9, 1958.

100. The *Asahi*, Tokyo, September 4, 1958, article entitled "Japan-China Problem and Our Political Parties," states: "The Suzuki main-current faction coldly brands Sata's visit to Red China as a failure. . . . the Nishio faction composed of Rightists, considering that the Chinese attitude revealed by the Sata report ignores the Japanese national feelings, insists that the Party should establish its attitude independently of the report."

101. See, for example, the article by Akira Doi, "International Background of the Japan-Communist China Trouble," *Nippon Oyobi Nippojin*, July 1958. Doi concludes: "At any rate, it can be said, I believe, that the focal point of the Japan-Communist China problem does not lie either in trade or the Nagasaki flag incident, but in the problem of American military bases in Japan."

102. At a banquet given for the Japanese delegation in Peiping on September 29, the Japanese delegate Yoshitaro Hirano stated: "The common struggle of the Japanese and Chinese people is for the withdrawal of the United States armed forces from Japan, Okinawa, and Taiwan." *NCNA*, Peiping, September 30, 1958.

103. For an interesting possibility on the reason for calling off the scheduled offensive against Taiwan in the spring of 1950, see Frank Kierman, "The Fluke that Saved Formosa," Center for International Studies, Massachusetts Institute of Technology, June 1, 1954. Chinese Communist troops of Lin Piao's Fourth Field Army actually started moving north away from the invasion coast opposite Taiwan even before the Korean War was launched by the Communists on June 25, 1950.

104. In October 1957, Chinese philosopher-statesman Dr. Hu Shih, spoke for the Chinese Delegation to the United Nations describing these events. His address which quoted from Communist mainland sources was entitled "Anti-Communist Revolts on Chinese Mainland," and was subsequently reprinted and issued by the Chinese-Canadian Cultural Association, Montreal in French and English.

105. *NCNA*, Peiping, July 3, 1958.

106. *Ta Kung Pao*, Peiping, July 4, 1958.

107. Peiping Radio in Mandarin to Taiwan, August 4, 1958.

108. The text of Khrushchev's letter is printed in *The New York Times*, September 9, 1958, p. 11.

109. The text of Pen Teh-huai's message on the suspension of bombardment was issued as a "Supplement" to the *Peking Review*, October 7, 1958.

110. Michael Lindsay, "Chinese Puzzle: Mao's Foreign Policy," *The New York Times Magazine*, October 12, 1958, pp. 7 and 78-81, the quotation is from pp. 80-81. Lord Lindsay spent six months in Taiwan in 1958 and reported more of his observations on conditions there in an article for the *New Republic*, "Formosa's Future," October 6, 1958, pp. 8-11.

112. *The New York Times*, October 16, 1958.

113. On Overseas Chinese affairs and plans, see *Current Background*, No. 390, No. 427 and No. 467; also *URS* of December 24, 1957 and the three issues of September 19, 23, and 25, 1958 entitled "Communist Menace to Hong Kong."

114. For a useful compendium of quotations from Mao and other top Chinese Communist leaders, from which these are taken, see Chiu Sin-min, "Some Basic Conceptions and Rules of Conduct of Chinese Communism," Lackland Air Force Base, Texas, January 1955.

115. Philip Selznick, *The Organizational Weapon: A Study of Bolshevik Strategy and Tactics*, New York, McGraw-Hill, 1952.

116. The free world has been slow in facing up to this two-edged organizational sword, but an impressive beginning was made at a special SEATO Seminar on Countering Communist Subversion held at Baguio, the Philippines, November 26-29, 1957. SEATO Headquarters in Bangkok, Thailand, subsequently published a report containing the major addresses made at the seminar.

117. Quoted in *The Asian Student*, weekly newspaper published by the Asia Foundation, San Francisco, October 16, 1956, p. 7.

118. This term is used in my article "Cultural Cold War in China," in a symposium entitled *Soviet Total War*, Committee on Un-American Activities, United States House of Representatives, September 30, 1956, pp. 764-767 which first presented some of the points elaborated in the discussion which follows. A more detailed treatment will be available in my chapter "The Developing Role of Cultural

Diplomacy in Asia," in the forthcoming *Issues and Conflicts,* University of Kansas Press, dealing with problems in twentieth century American diplomacy.

119. For a first-rate discussion of this same cultural strategy as directed toward newly developing countries by Moscow, see Frederick C. Barghoorn, "The New Cultural Diplomacy," *Problems of Communism,* 7.4, July-August, 1958.

120. For more detailed treatment of this aspect of Peiping's cultural cold war see my article "Guided Tourism in China," *Problems of Communism,* 6.5, September-October 1957. See also Evron M. Kirkpatrick's two excellent survey volumes on worldwide Communist propaganda: *Target: The World,* New York, Macmillan, 1956, and *Year of Crisis,* New York, Macmillan, 1957.

121. For an account of this see the reports from Belgrade by Elie Abel in *The New York Times* of June 10 and June 16, 1958.

122. Peiping Radio English broadcast to North America, June 11, 1958.

123. Tokyo, *Asahi,* December 14, 1957.

124. See, for example, the Tokyo *Yomiuri* of February 10, 1958 under the headline "Mao's Criticism of Kishi Administraiton Not Desirable," and the evening Tokyo *Shin Yukan* of February 23, 1958 under the headline "Japanese People Fooled by Red Nations." This article resents Chinese Communist implications that the Japanese people and their government are separate and antagonistic.

125. E. A. Reischauer, *Wanted: An Asian Policy,* New York, Knopf, 1955, pp. 174ff. The quotation is from p. 189. The assumption that there can be *an* Asian policy is reflective of the type of outlook referred to in Note 1.

126. Ricardo (pseud.), "China Realities," *FEER,* December 8, 1957.

127. David Rousset, "The Crisis in the Economic Structures of People's China," *FEER,* September 12, 1957.

128. V. I. Lenin, *Selected Works,* Moscow, Cooperative Publishing Society, 1935, Vol. IX, p. 242.

129. *The New York Times,* editorial, "The Basic Issue at Taiwan," September 10, 1958.

130. *Ta Kung Pao,* Peiping, June 23, 1958.

131. *People's Daily,* Peiping, October 13, 1958.

132. See, for example, *Peking Review,* August 26, 1958, pp. 19-20.

133. Address by Chou Yang at Tashkent, broadcast by Peiping Radio, October 11, 1958.

134. *The New York Times,* September 14, 1958. President Truman disagreed with members of his own party, including Adlai Stevenson, in urging the United States to remain firm in face of Chinese Communist blandishment.

135. Brian Crozier, "I Was Wrong about Free China," Pamphlet No. 3, published by the Friends of Free China Association, 62 New Cavendish Street, London, March 1957. The quotations are from p. 4. Crozier, upon his return to London, published two accounts of his visit in the *Economist,* and a transcript of his talk over BBC was published in *The Listener* of February 21, 1957. All three of these items together with a foreword are contained in the pamphlet.

136. See the *Chinese News Service,* 1270 Sixth Avenue, New York, "This Week in Free China,' 'January 31, 1956, p. 4.

PEIPING'S WORLD VIEW

[*Note:* The day after the close of the Second Session of the Eighth Congress of the Chinese Communist Party—May 5-24, 1958—the Central Committee met, and decided to launch publication of a new fortnightly theoretical journal, *Red Flag (Hung Ch'i)*. This journal, beginning with its first issue of June 1, for which Chairman Mao himself wrote a special article thus becomes the highest-ranking doctrinal journal in Communist China. Its editor, Ch'en Po-ta, is an alternate member of the Politburo, an arch Stalinist, and a ghost writer of some of Mao's reports. The following article from the August 16, 1958 issue of *Red Flag* thus carries the full and ominous weight of the Central Committee's view. In many respects it parallels an article which appeared in the *Current Affairs Journal (Shih-shih Shou-ts'e)* on November 5, 1950 shortly before the "Chinese People's Volunteers" entered Korea. That article was entitled "How to understand the United States," and one of its major points was: "Look with contempt upon the United States, for she is a paper tiger and can be fully defeated."

A close reading of this article should prove as eye-opening as it is grim, and perhaps the foregoing analysis will help to bring out some of its significant points. The article demonstrates how seriously Mao and his colleagues take their Leninist "newspeak" view of the world and the extent of their dedication to total Communist victory. It indicates their belief that their forces will gain from world-wide conflict, their faith in inevitability and infallibility. Certainly the article underscores the degree to which leaders in Peiping have talked themselves into a belief that the United States is weak and that nuclear weapons are unimportant. It highlights also their willingness to think in terms of the ultimate violence. Worth noting is the fact that the author has used some of the toughest quotes from Mao. Yü Chao-li is probably a pseudonym, quite possibly for Ch'en Po-ta himself, since the style of the article and the method of adducing quotations are very close to his.]

"The Forces of the New Are Bound to Defeat the Forces of Decay"

by Yü Chao-li

Developments in the current international situation further confirm Comrade Mao Tse-tung's famous dictum: "The east wind will prevail over the west wind." It is now abundantly clear that the forces of socialism are overwhelmingly superior to those of imperialism.

Imperialism is on its last legs. The First World War, which erupted as a result of the sharpened contradictions of world capitalism, showed that capitalism, after going through the process of birth and development, was headed down the road to decay and destruction.

The Great October Socialist Revolution ushered mankind into the new era of transition from capitalism to socialism. In the last four decades, the newborn revolutionary socialist forces have made enormous progress; the anti-imperialist national revolutionary forces, as the ally of the world socialist revolution, have also made great advances. These two forces have joined hands in one fierce struggle after another against the moribund forces of imperialism.

In the 20 years between the two world wars, imperialism for a time was able to suppress socialist revolutions and national revolutions in certain countries and thus give a temporary stability to the capitalist world. But it was not able to prevent the Soviet people from building socialism on one-sixth of the earth, nor did it have the strength to prevent the growth of revolutionary movements among the peoples in other countries.

Imperialism was powerless to hold off grave economic and political crises. The Second World War erupted as the inner contradictions of imperialism grew more acute than ever. In the 13 years since the end of the Second World War, imperialism has found itself in an even worse plight. It constantly finds itself in trouble as socialist revolutions and national revolutionary movements flare up in various parts of the world.

IMPERIALIST FORCES OUTNUMBERED

Today the last bastions of imperialism are being shaken violently by the irresistible popular revolutionary forces. The one billion people of the socialist camp now have at their side in the struggle against imperialism the more than 700 million people of the former colonial countries which have already won national independence. In addition, there are the 600 million people in the countries which are still fighting for full independence, and in capitalist countries which show neutralist tendencies. The imperialist countries have a combined population of only 400 millions, divided and at odds; everywhere beneath their feet there are volcanoes of revolt that may erupt at any moment.

In human history, the forces of the new always defeat the forces of decay. New, emergent forces, though seemingly weak, always prevail over the old, moribund forces which are still seemingly strong. What is decaying will inevitably be replaced by the newborn—such is the law of development in nature and in society.

The militia commanded by George Washington was weak, but eventually it defeated the well-armed British colonial troops. The revolutionary forces led by Dr. Sun Yat-sen were weak, but in the end they managed to overthrow the Manchu monarchy.

It is common knowledge that the Faysal monarchy, propped up as it was by the foreign imperialists, seemed to be quite strong even on the very eve of the outbreak of the Iraqi revolution, while the revolutionary strength of the people seemed weak. But overnight the forces of decay were defeated. The newborn forces of the Iraqi revolution won a resounding victory. Here was another convincing proof that the new must triumph over the old.

OLD FORCES FEAR NEW

This explains why it is the forces in decay who always fear the new, and not the other way around. Communists, in particular, are never afraid of imperialists; on the other hand, imperialists have always been afraid of communism. Over a hundred years ago, when the whole world was still under capitalist domination, a few Communists like Marx and Engels, barehanded as they were, were already bold enough to proclaim: "Let the ruling classes tremble at the Communist revolution. The proletarians have nothing to lose but their chains. They have a world to win."

Just after the October Revolution, when the Soviet state was still an isolated island encircled by the capitalist world, Lenin pointed out: ". . . The advanced, most civilized and 'democratic' countries—countries armed to the teeth and enjoying undivided military sway over the whole world—are mortally afraid of the ideological infection coming from a ruined, starving, backward, and even, as they assert, semi-savage country!" Under the slogan of "Victory is certain," Lenin mobilized the forces of the Soviet people and defeated the armed intervention launched by the so-called first-class great powers.

In our country, the two forces of imperialism and

feudalism once loomed like mountains and lorded it over the
people, but the vanguard of the Chinese working class, en-
lightened by Marxism-Leninism and guided by Comrade Mao
Tse-tung, already saw the future clearly and was fully confident that the newborn forces of the people would be able to
overthrow these towering obstacles.

Immediately after it was founded, the Chinese Communist Party courageously raised the slogan of opposing imperialism and feudalism. The revolution suffered setbacks,
but the Chinese Communists trusted firmly in the truth stated
by Comrade Mao Tse-tung: "A single spark can start a prairie
fire!"

CHIANG ATTACK HASTENED DEFEAT

Twelve years ago, the U.S. imperialists and the Chiang
Kai-shek clique, with its fully armed regular army of 4 million
men, launched a ferocious attack against the forces of the
Chinese people, which at that time were split up among
dozens of bases and had a poorly equipped liberation army of
around a million men. But Comrade Mao Tse-tung predicted
that aggressor and dictator were digging their own graves; he
pointed out that their attacks would lead to an early victory
of the Chinese revolution.

This is how history treads the paths of revolutionary
dialectics. The old world will eventually be replaced by the
new world.

In his talk with the American correspondent Anna
Louise Strong in 1956, Comrade Mao Tse-tung made the
famous statement "All reactionaries are paper tigers." "The
reactionaries look formidable, but actually their strength is
not so great. Taking the long view, it is the people, not the
reactionaries, who are really powerful." "The U.S. reactionaries," he added, "are also paper tigers. . . . Like all reactionaries in history, they will be proved to be quite powerless."

In the last 12 years, we have witnessed the victories of

the socialist revolutions in the Eastern European people's democracies, the victory of the people's revolutionary war and socialist revolution in China, the victory of the struggle for national independence in India, Burma and Indonesia, the victory of the war of resistance to U.S. aggression in Korea, the victory of the revolutionary war of the Vietnamese people against the U.S.-French imperialists, the victory of national independence movements in North Africa and West Asia, the victory in the war against the Anglo-French seizure of the Suez Canal in Egypt, the victory of national independence movements in Latin American countries, the victory gained in preserving national independence, opposing imperialist aggression and smashing the rebel forces in Indonesia, the victory of the Syrian people's struggle against imperialism, and the recent victory of the peoples of the Middle and Near East in their fight against U.S.-British imperalist aggression and the struggle to preserve their national independence and freedom. All these are incontrovertible proof of the fact that the imperialists and reactionaries in the various countries are truly paper tigers.

U.S. RALLIES "CERTAIN WAVERERS"

Today, that paper tiger—U.S. reaction—despite its holes and tatters, is still trying to give itself airs and talking big in an attempt both to cover up its own panic and scare certain waverers. The policy pursued by the U.S. reactionaries is a militaristic and aggressive one. They have established over 250 military bases in the vast intermediate areas around the socialist countries; they have wooed the reactionaries in more than 20 countries, patched together several military blocs, and constantly create tension and carry on war propaganda.

But all this, far from showing their strength, is a sign of their weakness. Although the U.S. bourgeoisie has a history of less than 200 years, it has long since forsaken the banner of independence and freedom raised by Washington, Jefferson, and Lincoln. Rotten to the core, it is beyond recovery. At home it owes its dominance to McCarthyism and the Un-American Activities Committee.

As for foreign policy, the U.S. imperialists have rallied all the reactionary forces of the capitalist world to their banner; they have become the center of world reaction and made themselves the enemy of all the world's people, of world peace and the national independence movement. As a result, they are extremely isolated. They can find support only among a handful of reactionary elements, while the people of the world and all peace-loving countries are against them. In pursuing this reactionary policy they are digging their own graves, hell-bent to ruin.

The fate of Hitler and all such warlike elements awaits the U.S. imperialist aggressive bloc. Worse than that, Hitler was for a time fairly successful in his aggressive adventures, for then the forces supporting peace and against aggression were relatively weak. Not so for U.S. imperialism today. In its armed aggression against Lebanon, the moment its troops landed on the Beirut seafront, it found itself in a quandary. The imperialist aggressors are condemned and opposed by the people everywhere; they have met with the valiant resistance of the peoples of the Arab countries, who have the support of the socialist countries and all the other forces of peace throughout the world. The members of the imperialist aggressive bloc themselves are seriously at loggerheads; there are splits inside the ruling groups in the United States and Britain.

U.S. IMPERIALISTS ISOLATED

The U.S. imperialists are isolated as never before. Confronted as they are by the powerful socialist camp and people in all lands who treasure peace and freedom, the imperialists are overextended on too long a front; they lack the necessary strength and are vulnerable at many points. Now, when it really comes to brandishing its arms, the imperialist aggressive bloc that once made such a continuous hullabaloo about a third world war, is shaking in its shoes and worrying about its future.

The hue and cry against the Soviet Union and communism raised by the U.S. imperialists is in fact a smoke screen under cover of which they are invading and enslaving the countries in the intermediate region between the socialist camp and the United States of America. The United States is separated from the socialist countries by whole oceans; almost the entire capitalist world lies between them. To start a war against the Soviet Union, U.S. imperialism must first bring this capitalist world to its knees. In order to set up military bases in a country, the U.S. imperialists must first invade that country. They build military bases everywhere, so they carry out aggression everywhere, so they are naturally everywhere encircled by the people.

It is common knowledge that U.S. imperialism, in dealing with the countries in the vast region between the socialist camp and itself, resorts to both secret and open plots, to force and "peaceful means." But today, when there exist a powerful socialist camp and the other forces of world peace, the aggressive war policies of the imperialists must inevitably suffer one setback after another.

Many facts prove that today superiority rests with the socialist camp headed by the Soviet Union, not with the imperialist camp headed by the United States; with the Communist parties and other progressive social forces in the various countries which truly represent the interests of the peoples of those countries, not with the reactionary ruling classes that oppose the will of the people; with the peace-loving countries and peoples of the world, and not with the handful of warmongers.

OPPRESSED NATIONS TRIUMPH

Today, it is the Arab people who have the upper hand, not the United States, Britain and France; Indonesia, not the United States and Holland; the Algerian forces of the national liberation movement, not the French reactionaries who cling to colonial rule; the Iraqi Republic, not the imperialist aggressive forces. Imperialism is like the setting sun in the west; socialism and the national liberation movements supported by it are like the rising sun in the east. It is difficult for the imperialists to subvert the nationalist countries which have already won independence, and they are not in a position to hold back the further progress of the national liberation movements in Asia, Africa and Latin America.

The imperialist aggressive bloc always attempts to use war to frighten the people of the world. The people do not want war and oppose it. As long as all the peace-loving forces of the world are united in an active struggle to defend peace, war can be prevented.

WAR WILL HASTEN IMPERIALIST END

However, as the communique on the recent talks between Comrades Mao Tse-tung and N. S. Khrushchev pointed out, ". . . whether war can be avoided does not rest with the good will and one-sided efforts of the peace-loving peoples alone. The aggressive bloc of the Western powers has up to now refused to take any serious steps to save peace but, on the contrary, is aggravating international tension unscrupulously, thus bringing mankind to the brink of the catastrophe of war. It should know, however, that if the imperialist war maniacs should dare to impose war on the people of the world, all the countries and peoples who love peace and freedom will unite closely to wipe out clean the imperialist aggressors and so establish everlasting world peace."

This is a penetrating judgment concerning the development of the present world situation. As an old Chinese saying has it: "War is like fire; if you don't quench it, you'll get burned yourself." Lenin once said that there was no phenomenon that would not turn into its opposite—as an imperialist war can be turned into a revolutionary war.

If the imperialists insist on war, the people will certainly study politics more closely in a war they are forced to fight and will quickly raise their level of political consciousness; they will never continue to tolerate a system that brings them such endless sufferings and sacrifices; they will rise in their anger and hurl the imperialist aggressive bloc into its grave.

ATOMIC BOMB IS PAPER TIGER

The U.S. reactionaries try to use nuclear weapons to scare people. They brag about the horrors of atomic and hydrogen bombs to bluff and deceive everywhere. But even when the atomic bomb first made its appearance and was still the monopoly of the U.S. reactionaries, Comrade Mao Tsetung described it scathingly as a "paper tiger." He said: "The atomic bomb is a paper tiger. It looks as if it is a fearful thing; it is not so as a matter of fact. . . . The emergence of the atomic bomb marks the beginning of the end of U.S. imperialism. The reason is because it relies on nothing but bombs. But in the end the bomb will not destroy the people. The people will destroy the bomb."

Marxists have always maintained that it is the man behind the gun that counts. Whenever and wherever monarchies were overthrown or aggressors defeated, it was not because they did not have what were considered at the time to be the most dreadful weapons; on the contrary, so far as weapons were concerned they always enjoyed the advantage. To the people who fought barehanded against monarchical authority in the past, swords, spears, bows and arrows were the ancient equivalents of "atomic bombs."

To the Chinese people's armed forces in the revolutionary bases who had "only rifles and millet," the complete
arsenal of weapons and equipment possessed by the imperialists and their lackeys could also be regarded as the "atomic
weapons" of that time. The reactionaries killed tens of thousands of the Chinese people, but finally the Chinese people
disposed of all these "paper tigers."

The U.S. policy of atomic blackmail has never daunted
the revolutionary people. Furthermore, a U.S. monopoly of
nuclear weapons has long been a thing of the past. In the
socialist camp, the Soviet Union has long since been in posses-
sion of nuclear weapons, and in the field of some of the most
important branches of military science and technology, such
as intercontinental ballistic missiles, has left the United States
far behind.

PEACE CAMP CAN PREVENT WAR

The fact that "the east wind prevails over the west
wind" is the basic condition for preventing the outbreak of
atomic war. The socialist camp is dedicated to peace and
firmly believes that the forces defending peace can prevent
the outbreak of atomic war.

But we must keep a watchful eye on the atomic war
maniacs. There is only one way to deal with madmen—to
expose and fight them. Only when everybody is on the alert
and gives them no chance to run amok can such madmen be
held down when they are seized with the fit to take some mad
action. Those who want to run amok must be told that once
they start an atomic war, the result will be the destruction of
imperialism, which has brought untold suffering to mankind.
Socialism, far from being destroyed, will be realized all the
more quickly throughout the world.

The U.S. reactionaries have indulged in sabre-rattling
in every part of the world, thinking that the United States,
with its annual output of over 100 million tons of steel, still

for the time being ranks first in the world in output of steel and a number of other important industrial products. But this should scare no one. Steel is important, but man is much more important. Even in steel the United States does not enjoy an absolute superiority. Not until the early part of the 20th century did the United States complete its industrialization and become capable of producing 20 to 30 million tons of steel a year. That was 130 to 140 years after it gained independence and 40 to 50 years after its civil war. Another 40 years passed before it increased its annual steel output to over 100 million tons. This increase was made mainly as a result of the two world wars. Relying mainly on war instead of on a dependable domestic market, the increase of steel output in the United States is actually built on sand.

U.S. INDUSTRIAL LEAD IRRELEVANT

The decaying U.S. capitalist system is not going to be saved by 100 million tons of steel; it cannot escape from its fatal economic crises. The current economic crisis in the United States actually started with the steel industry and the industrial branches directly associated with it. Steel output in the United States in the first quarter of this year went down 40 percent compared with the same period of last year. During the 1929-1933 crisis, the memory of which is still fresh, steel output in the United States fell sharply from 57 million tons to 13.9 million tons. For the U.S. monopoly capitalists, the higher they climb, the harder they will fall.

There is no element of life known that can cure the fatal disease of economic crisis with which the United States is afflicted. It is man and the superiority of a social system which play the decisive part in history.

During the antifascist war, the annual steel output of the Soviet Union amounted to only 18 million tons. Besides, the country suffered heavy war damage. The steel output of the United States and Britain then added up to more than 70 million tons. But it was the Soviet Union, rather than the United States and Britain, which played the decisive role in winning the war against Hitler.

In the race of the artificial earth satellites, which represent the pinnacle of the world's scientific achievement, it is the Soviet Union, whose annual steel output is 50 million tons, rather than the United States with its annual steel output of over 100 million tons, which has won first prize.

As to the rate of increase of steel output, the Soviet Union is more than a match for the United States. During the 12 years since the Second World War the steel output of the Soviet Union soared from approximately 10 million tons a year to more than 50 million tons. At this rate it will very quickly catch up with and surpass the United States.

Apart from the Soviet Union, the steel output and other branches of industrial and agricultural production in many other socialist countries too are expanding swiftly. The constant leaps in production in the socialist world stand in sharp contrast with the economic crisis of the capitalist world headed by the United States. As is well known, the swift rate of expansion of the iron and steel industry in China will also surpass people's expectations.

In the eyes of the Chinese people, the United States with its 100 million tons of steel a year is no better than Yüan Shu and his like described by Ts'ao Ts'ao in his "Discussion on Contemporary Heroes" [an episode from the well-known classic novel, *Romance of the Three Kingdoms*]. Although it still has "large numbers of soldiers and ample supplies" at its disposal, just as Yüan Shu had in his time, U.S. imperialism already has one foot in the grave and can, with as much justice, be described as "a rotting bone in a graveyard."

SETBACKS STRENGTHEN REVOLUTIONISTS

The imperialists and the reactionaries in various countries always stir up anti-Soviet and anti-Communist disturbances the better to suppress their own peoples and the revolutionary movements in their own countries. But this can only scare the weak-kneed.

The revolutionary people, on their part, will be tempered in these tempests and emerge stronger than ever. All revolutionary forces are born and grow on the strength of two factors: on the one hand, they need positive revolutionary education; on the other, counterrevolutionaries can serve in reverse as educators. The more reactionary their enemies become, the greater revolutionary fervor the people will acquire and the faster their enemies will go to their doom.

Indomitable Communists and all revolutionaries grow to maturity amid stress and storms, which provide them with the opportunity of getting to know the laws of waging the struggle against the reactionaries. At times temporary losses may occur owing to lack of experience in fighting the imperialists and the reactionaries, but losses help you to learn. As the Chinese saying goes: "A fall in the pit, a gain in wit." And that is why bad things can be turned to good account.

Comrade Mao Tse-tung said at the time of the victory of the Chinese people's revolution in 1949 that the logic of the imperialists was different from the logic of the people. Troublemaking, defeat, troublemaking again, defeat again, and finally destruction—this is the logic that guides the imperialists and all reactionaries. Under no circumstances will they run counter to this logic. This is a Marxist-Leninist truth. On the other hand, struggle, failure, struggle again, failure again, and finally victory—this is the logic of the people. They, too, will not run counter to this logic. This is another Marxist-Leninist truth.

Both the Russian People's revolution and the Chinese People's revolution bear this out. Some decades ago, there existed in Russia and China only a few Marxist groups formed by a few dozen people. They weathered temporary failures and waged fresh struggles; finally they defeated all the outwardly strong reactionaries and became the parties in power in these two great countries. This is revolutionary dialectics.

IMPERIALIST DOOM FOREORDAINED

The world situation today is one in which "the strong winds foretell the coming storm." None of the imperialist reactionaries who still seem outwardly strong can avoid the doom ordained by history. The Communist parties in these countries, which still appear to be weak, are the truly mighty forces to be reckoned with; they will grow and gain in strength in the course of their struggles, and will eventually triumph.

Ten years ago, Comrade Mao Tse-tung pointed out: "To underestimate the significance of the victory of the Second World War will be a great mistake." He also said: "To overestimate the strength of our enemies and underestimate the revolutionary forces will be a great mistake."

This equally applies to the appraisal of forces at this new historical turning point today. The situation in which the east wind prevails over the west wind has paved the way for the final victory of the struggles of the peoples the world over. No force can turn back the fast-moving wheel of history. The newborn forces will certainly defeat the forces of decay. The speed of advance of the forces of peace, democracy, and socialism will certainly surpass the people's expectations.

THE PEOPLE'S COMMUNES

[*Note:* The following two documents illustrate how the Peiping authorities have linked their movement for people's communes to the world struggle and also the degree to which the movement is a concerted attack on the Chinese family. In the first article from the *People's Daily* the enthusiasm of the author fails to obscure most of the realities of life on the commune, such as, for example, the fact that the mate of an 87-year-old peasant should be returning from the night shift in the fields at midnight. The second document is in many respects much more frightening. It spells out the full implications of the commune revolution in the Chinese countryside in unmistakable terms. The Chinese family is to be eliminated. Mao Tse-tung was obviously in dead earnest when he said that the only true love is class love.]

1.]

"Beautiful Prospects and Graves"

by K'ang Cho

From the People's Daily *of August 6, 1958*

While American and British imperialism is engaged in aggression against Middle East countries, we are living in beautiful surroundings in the countryside where buds of Communism are sprouting everywhere.

China is moving forward at the speed of space flight. Not long ago, peasants who were in their fifties were worried because they might not last long enough to see the good days of Communism. Now even the octogenarians and nonagenarians cheerfully and firmly believe that they can enjoy the happiness of Communism. Some old men even firmly believe that they are already living in an age of Communism. The old husband of Aunt Hsieh Kuo-chen of Tassukochuang, Hsushui *hsien* [county] is 87 years old this year. Some days ago, when the village power plant began to produce electricity, he went out to the brightly lit street at midnight one night and sat there alone, refusing to go to bed. His old mate, returning home from a night shift in the fields, was astonished to find him still up so late and urged him to go home. He said to her:

"You go home first if you feel sleepy. I want to taste Communism here!"

Of course, generation of power does not amount to Communism, but there is a great deal of truth in what the 87-year-old man said. Like all other agricultural cooperatives in Hsushui *hsien,* Tassukochuang has had its communal kitchens and mess halls for some time. One of the mess halls is for the exclusive use of children and the aged, who enjoy certain privileges. A nursery was also set up a long time ago; the children in the nursery are supported, not by their own parents, but by the cooperative. More important still, private plots of land have been abolished and all grave mounds have been levelled in Tassukochuang as in all other places in the *hsien.* All the pigs are fed and kept by the cooperative. All the old and dilapidated houses and kitchen ranges have been pulled down. Unfired bricks are used in the fields, while the better grades of bricks are being used for building houses. The houses, when completed, will be allocated according to the number of people in a household and not according to the number of rooms formerly occupied by each household. The supply and marketing cooperative and credit cooperative have become part of the agricultural cooperative. Work in this respect, following the abolition of fairs throughout the *hsien*, is gradually reducing the gap between the urban and the rural areas. The agricultural cooperative also owns over a dozen machines. There are factories for food processing and making fertilizer. There is also a sewing department and a barber shop. Following the overall adjustment of land, management of the fields has become specialized as has the management of factories. The crops grow wonderfully well under this system of management. Soon the club house will have lantern slide shows, broadcasting, books, music, and everything. In a word, new buds of Communism are sprouting in Tassukochuang and everywhere in Hsushui. The system of people's communes, which are impregnated with Communism, is beginning to take concrete shape here. Who would have thought one year ago, or even a few months ago, that such a perfect ideal could be realized within such a short time? The Party's general line and the magnificent, inexhaustible creative power of the Chinese people are enabling us to live not merely twenty years, but two hundred or even two thousand years, in a day.

I do not intend to dwell any longer on the beautiful prospects of Tassukochuang. However, I have to mention here once more the time when electric power first became available there. It is the first rural power plant in Hsushui. On the night of July 18, the *hsien* authorities held a 10,000-man meeting to celebrate the completion of the power plant. As soon as the plant started sending out current, all the electric lights in the place went on, and all at once the hearts of the 300,000 people of the *hsien* were lit up and glowed with warmth. It was a joyful rally of deafening cheers. But soon the joyful cheers turned into a roaring sea of wrath as the 10,000 people who gathered there raised their arms, shouted slogans against the American and British imperialist aggression against the Middle East and pledged themselves to support with all their might the struggle of their Arab brethren.

The boundless wrath reached the skies. It was not only the noise and the fervor of the people. They were encouraged by the beautiful prospect of electrification and angered by the piratical acts of the imperialist powers. People immediately took action. They are trying to excel themselves. Tassuko-chuang agricultural cooperative has led the rest by raising its target of 10,000 catties [1.102 lb.] of grain per *mow* [1/6 acre] this year to 15,000 catties per *mow*. A number of *hsiang* [administrative villages] are already producing 10,000 catties per *mow*. The people have guaranteed higher yields per *mow* and higher yields over large areas, so that they may overtake Britain and the United States in production sooner and give support to the Arab people. The piratical acts of the imperialist powers stand in sharp contrast with the electrification of rural China. The electric lights inflame the people's fervor, while the black deeds of the pirates anger them so that they work all the harder.

The increase in fervor for work is not confined to Tassukochuang. Thousands of cities and rural districts all over the world are in a great leap forward in construction like Tassukochuang. There are millions and millions of people who have already shaken off or are shaking off the yoke of colonialism, and there are millions and millions of people in the capitalist countries too, who are fighting for peace and democracy. All these people are vehemently protesting and taking practical action against the crimes of the American and British pirates and are giving support to their Arab brethren. In the people's camp the population is larger, the people are willing to work, they have justice, they have the best weapons, and therefore are like the rising sun. The imperialist powers, on the other hand, can make a stand in no department at all. The pirates are like the setting sun, and their mad aggression is like its parting glare. The royal rulers of Iraq, whom the imperialist powers painstakingly brought up, have been overthrown by the people in less than two hours. That shows that

the pirates are collapsing at a flying speed. There is no future
for imperialism, and where it starts aggression there its grave
will be. In rural China, grave mounds are being levelled and
public cemeteries built. But the body of imperialism has no
right to be buried in a people's public cemetery. There is no
place for a cemetery for imperialism. Imperialism will find no
place to bury itself!

2.]

"COLLECTIVIZATION AND SOCIALIZATION OF DOMESTIC WORK"
by Hu Shen

(The following is a summary of an article from Red
Flag, *the official theoretical journal of the Central Committee
of the Chinese Communist Party, as broadcast by Peiping
radio for its Latin American listeners.)*

At the present time dining rooms, laundries, mills,
nurseries, and day nurseries are being set up everywhere in
the rural zones. For generations tasks such as preparation of
food, care of children, sewing, repair of shoes, laundry, and so
on have been done by each family separately, especially in
peasant homes.

How could the peasants break with the old tradition
and introduce innovations such as nurseries, day nurseries,
and so on?

This could be done in connection with cooperation in
agricultural tasks. When peasants work on individual parcels
of land, domestic tasks are also performed separately in each
home. This happens because on small farms the peasants can
never see themselves free from poverty. They must solve
various problems of daily life by their own efforts, within
their own families.

Agricultural cooperation promoted the liberation of
productive efforts in agriculture. The great advantages of
cooperation became evident, a great increase in agricultural

production took place. This increase, in turn, demands the removal of everything that obstructs the development of the productive strength of society.

Although the preparation of food, sewing, the milling of grain, and other similar tasks became collective work, resulting in a great saving in labor, there were tasks which were still performed individually. When these tasks were collectivized, their total mechanization or semimechanization was made possible.

As an example, let us take the preparation of food. The network of public dining rooms in Hunan totaled 280,000 in June this year. The peasants are thoroughly convinced of the advantages of collectivization. For the first time, after centuries and millennia, the aspect of domestic tasks has changed completely. This change resulted in the following:

    1—A great number of women were liberated from enslaving household chores, making it possible for them to devote themselves to productive and social work based on equality with men.

    2—Despite this liberation, people were still needed for domestic chores. However, since the collectivization of this type of work, the social position of the persons doing this work has changed radically.

The explanation for this is to be found in the fact that there are no longer household chores, but social work, equal to that of factories and agricultural cooperatives.

When these tasks were done within the family, the women were completely absorbed by them, and thus were oppressed and relegated to a secondary place. Now, however, when the women work in public dining rooms, nurseries, sewing workshops, and so on, the work develops their abilities and their political growth. From among them, advanced workers can emerge just as in any other branch of production.

These changes are taking place not only in the rural areas, but also in urban zones, in workers' neighborhoods, and so on. The people say, and they are right, this means new liberation for women. Without taking such a step, the total liberation of women is not possible.

The victory of democratic revolution and the victory of socialist transformation have liberated large groups of women from the political and economic yoke under which they lived in the old society. However, the complete liberation of women has not yet taken place.

Lenin said that true liberation of women, true Communism, begins only when and where the mass struggle begins against the small domestic economy, or even better, when its massive reorganization occurs on the basis of socialist economy.

The peasant women of China, by their own experience, have demonstrated the truth of Lenin's words. They say that since nurseries, day nurseries, public dining rooms, and so on were organized, they have begun to be liberated from the fate which previously forced them to spend the whole day over the fire and the washtub and at sewing and milling. This means that only now they have become truly free women.

In collectivizing and socializing domestic tasks we have achieved the liberation of Chinese women, which constitute one-half of our country's 600 million inhabitants. They have been freed from the tiresome domestic chores, and it is now possible for them to fully join society's productive work, increase their political activity, their cultural level, and fully develop their abilities, talents, and strength. This is a measure of extraordinary importance in the socialist construction of our country.

The way of life tied to private property, which has been dragging along for thousands of years, and in which each family, separately, is considered to be the basis of society, makes slaves of people and engenders a selfish mentality in them. Maintenance of that type of life for people, without any change, inhibits collective socialist production and does not promote socialist production development; on the contrary, it prevents the effective stabilizing of the people's standard of living and prevents the development of socialist and Communist ideology. The time to change this manner of living is at hand.

It is possible that the question will be raised: "Will this not lead to the destruction of the family?" In response to this question, it is necessary to point out that the family has a different role from the viewpoint of the various stages of the historical development of humanity and from that of various classes of society.

Let us consider, for example, the feudal society in our country. Life for the exploiters was very different from that of the exploited. In the house of the exploiter all the happiness and good in the material and spiritual aspects were gathered. He lived as he wanted to live. For the exploited, the family was a prison cell. Peasants worked the land with their sweat in order to feed the parasites who lived at their expense, and could hardly provide the minimum of food required for their own families. Therefore, it can be said that the family of exploiters was a unit for the enjoyment of life, while the family of the exploited was a unit for work and production. These feudal families were destroyed by capitalism.

However, the bourgeois family continued, as before, to be a family of exploiters who lived a parasitic life. In addition, the bourgeoisie did not limit itself to the enjoyment of family life. For greater enjoyment, they created theaters, clubs, restaurants, great hotels, educational institutions, parks, gambling houses, and brothels—all this was to make the life of the bourgeoisie more comfortable.

On the other hand, capitalism brought greater poverty to the peasants and small producers, making possible family work of oppression. In this manner, capitalism created an army of salaried workers, including the cheap labor of women. Many peasants were forced to leave their homes, their own regions. Many poor people in towns were left homeless. They had to satisfy their hunger with whatever they could find. Many mothers had to leave their children in orphanages, and many even had to desert their children in desperation.

In the capitalist society, the life of the people is also socialized, but this socialization means that the rich have all they want while the poor exist in the most miserable living conditions.

From the above, it can be seen that with private control over the means of production and with the exploitation of man by man, the role of the family is of little consequence. The family institution existed only for the exploiters.

If we want to destroy the traditional family, it is necessary to understand that this destruction, by its nature, is radically different from the destruction of the family by capitalism. We want to destroy the bourgeois social life, based on the system of class exploitation, and the family based on the system of class exploitation.

Regarding exploiting classes, we have carried out an enormous destructive task. It is natural that it is necessary to destroy the parasitic life that lives on the basis of others' work. Regarding workers' families, we have only destroyed the family which was a miserable cell, the prison of the worker.

We have completely changed the destiny of workers who lacked a true home under the conditions of the capitalist regimes.

In the socialist society the worry of not being able to support one's family will no longer exist. Therefore, we say that while capitalism destroyed the worker's family, socialism allows the workers to create their families anew. However, people cannot return to the past and live the old type of family life based on the system of individual production, but must organize a new era under conditions of socialist property.

Our people will live a cultured, high-quality life. People will not only develop social production with collective forces, but with collective forces will create a higher and more cultured life for society. In a socialist and Communist society, everyone works with joy and makes use of the fruits of work in a reasonable manner. Although it is clear that the family made up of a husband, a wife, and children will still exist for a long time, the full life of the people will spill out of the framework of the family, and then the past will be removed, never to return to a family which is backward in the cultural field, to a family which never knew anything but work, hunger, and cold. And in the same manner the families of the parasitic classes, which live at the expense of the work of others, will also belong to a past that will never return.

COMMUNIST PRESSURES AGAINST THE BRITISH IN HONG KONG

[*Note:* When, on August 26, 1958, British authorities closed the Communist-run Chung Hua Middle School in Hong Kong, mainland authorities used the occasion to resume threats against the crown colony. The Peking Foreign Office delivered an official protest to the British charge d'affaires, and this was buttressed by additional protests presented by mass organizations couched in almost identical language. These organizations then conducted demonstrations against the British in major Chinese cities through the end of August and beginning of September. It will be recalled that this was at the very moment when Communist shelling of Quemoy and other offshore islands, which started August 23, was reaching its peak.

The following two items illustrate the Communist attempt to apply pressure on the British. The first contains excerpts from one of the protests delivered to the British representative in Peking, and the second is the editorial from the *People's Daily* of August 28, 1958

There are more than a million strongly anti-Communist Chinese refugees in Hong Kong, and they have relied on British firmness and protection to prevent mainland pressures and threats against them from getting out of hand. Peking's attempts to organize the youth, control the schools, spread propaganda through special night classes, and seize the labor unions in Hong Kong have frequently exploited the precarious position of the British there and the obvious difficulty of maintaining this center of freedom bordering on the lands of a Communist regime which the British recognize and with whom they attempt to carry on normal relations. Peking's willingness to use all sorts of pressures against Hong Kong without any hesitation about the fact that their actions constitute internal interference in British territory offers a clue not only to plans for exploiting and controlling overseas Chinese but also of ultimate intent to seize Hong Kong. In the face of such threats the British have performed a remarkable feat for humanity in maintaining this secure refuge for the thousands of Chinese who continue to stream from the Communist regime every month.

It is worth noting that for several days, beginning August 27, 1958, the Chinese Communist internal press gave preponderant attention to the Hong Kong crisis rather than to Quemoy and the Taiwan Strait area which so deeply concerned the rest of the world. Threats against Hong Kong authorities and denunciations of the "outrageous," "barbarous," "provocative," actions as well as promises of "just revenge" for a "blood debt" to the British received practically no attention abroad even in the British home press which was also more concerned with Quemoy.]

*   *   *

1. *Excerpts from protest of the All-China Students' Federation handed to the British charge d'affaires in Peking, August 27, 1958.*

On behalf of all Chinese students we express our extreme indignation at your ferocious action and raise our strong protest and serious warning to the British Government. . . . It was by no means accidental that the British authorities in Hong Kong forcibly closed the premises of the Chung Hua Middle School . . . they allowed schools run by U.S. and Chiang Kai-shek special agents to hang the flag of the Chiang Kai-shek clique every day. Moreover, they forced all schools to teach from reactionary textbooks published by the Chiang

Kai-shek clique. Recently they forcibly expelled Parker Tu, the headmaster of the Pei Chiao Middle School from Hong Kong. These series of cases show that the British authorities in Hong Kong are deliberately persecuting the Chinese people's educational work.

Not only that, the British authorities in Hong Kong have always sheltered the espionage organizations of the Chiang Kai-shek clique, deadly foes of the Chinese people, and allowed Hong Kong to be used as a base to conduct sabotage activities against new China.

We have not forgotten during the riots in Kowloon two years ago, the connivance of the British authorities in Hong Kong with Kuomintang special agents and thugs in killing and plundering our compatriots in Hong Kong and Kowloon.

All these facts completely expose the attitude of the British Government, as hostile to the Chinese people and aiming at creating "two Chinas".

We seriously warn the British Government that it must immediately stop its persecution of the Chinese people's educational work in Hong Kong, reasonably solve the problem of the premises of the Chung Hua Middle School at once, so that schooling can be carried on in time; severely punish all the criminals, compensate for all losses suffered by the Chung Hua Middle School; and ensure that there will be no similar cases in the future.

If the British authorities in Hong Kong persist in their present course and continue to ignore the Chinese people's grave warning, then they must bear responsibility for all the consequences.

2. People's Daily *"Editorial," August 28, 1958.*

Sending in a big force of armed police the Hong Kong British authorities on August 26 forcibly closed down the

Chung Hua Middle School in Hong Kong and indiscriminately beat up the teachers and students of the school and the Chinese reporters who were covering the news. The news of this event has aroused the Chinese people to great indignation. It is an addition to the list of criminal actions committed by the Hong Kong British authorities in their hostility to the Chinese people. We strongly protest against this.

The persecution of Chung Hua Middle School by the Hong Kong British authorities is not an isolated event. It is part of the planned efforts of the Hong Kong British authorities to deliberately suppress the patriotic educational undertakings of the Chinese people in Hong Kong and Kowloon. At the beginning of January this year, the Hong Kong British authorities published a reactionary "education ordinance" in face of resolute opposition among educational circles and other sections of the people in Hong Kong and Kowloon. They then carried out a series of attacks on the patriotic undertakings of the Chinese people in Hong Kong and Kowloon. On February 1, on the pretext of an infringement of the "education ordinance," they sentenced two staff members of the literacy class run by the Tsing Shan Branch of the Planters' Association and at the same time searched the premises of other literacy classes. Again, on May 1, using the absurd excuse that the "education ordinance" provided for a ban on flying so-called "political and semi-political" flags by schools, they overbearingly and unreasonably interfered with the Han Hua Middle School and eight other schools who flew China's national flag. On May 10, they prohibited the Hsin Chiao Middle School from flying the national flag of China and singing the national anthem. On July 29, they forced the Wen Ming School to close down on the excuse that its premises were dilapidated and not fit for use. On August 6, they forcibly removed without cause Parker Tu, Principal of the Pei Chiao Middle School, from Hong Kong. All this interference and persecution, carried out on the pretext that "politics should not be introduced into schools," in effect was directed at preventing the Chinese people from expressing their love for their motherland and banning patriotic education from the Chinese people's schools in Hong Kong and Kowloon. On the other hand, the Hong Kong British authorities permit the schools run by the U.S.-Chiang Kai-shek espionage service to fly the flag of the Chiang Kai-shek clique every day and unbridled, political propaganda slandering China to be conducted there by "teachers" belonging to the Chiang Kai-shek special service. In particular, the Hong Kong British authorities have gone to the lengths of stipulating that the schools in Hong Kong and Kowloon must adopt textbooks published in Taiwan or by the U.S.-Chiang espionage service in Hong Kong. Is not the intent and purpose of all this clear enough? All the claptrap about "politics should not be introduced into the schools" is explicit political trickery to create a "two Chinas" situation.

It is in no way accidental that the Hong Kong British authorities are trying to suppress the patriotic educational undertakings of the Chinese people in Hong Kong and Kowloon. It is a further demonstration of the fact that the British Government and the Hong Kong authorities have all along been toeing the line of the United States in its hostile attitude to New China and the Chinese people.

Shielded and pampered by the Hong Kong British authorities, the U.S.-Chiang Kai-shek special servicemen have long been using Hong Kong as a stronghold from which they carry out various kinds of sabotage against our country. Moreover, the Hong Kong British authorities acquiesce in the use of Hong Kong by the Chiang Kai-shek clique of Taiwan as a base from which to conduct armed harassment of China's mainland. Of late, in coordination with the efforts of the U.S. and its Chiang Kai-shek hirelings to create tension in the Far East and the Taiwan Straits, Britain has not only allowed U.S. troops to land at Singapore but has turned Hong

Kong into a haunt for them. It has even sent its military aircraft stationed in Hong Kong to intrude over our territorial air, for reconnaissance and harassment. It was in these very serious circumstances that the Hong Kong British authorities set their armed police on to brutally attack totally unarmed Chinese teachers, students and newspapermen. The Chinese people necessarily regard this as a flagrant, deliberate, provocative outrage on the part of the Hong Kong British authorities.

Our Ministry of Foreign Affairs on August 27 sent two notes to the British Government, one lodging a protest against the intrusion by British military aircraft over our territorial air and the other lodging a protest against the action of the Hong Kong British authorities in suppressing the educational undertakings of the Chinese people in Hong Kong and Kowloon and setting their police to beat up Chinese teachers, students and journalists. We fully support these protests, which express the wrath of the 600 million Chinese people. Furthermore, we warn the British Government and the Hong Kong British authorities, now that the aggressive activities of the U.S. and British imperialists in the Middle and Near East have been frustrated by the rebuff given by the peace-loving countries and peoples all over the world—if the British Government collaborates with U.S. imperialism in continuing to create tension in the Far East—we can say with certainty that it will come to no happy end. Up to this moment, the Chinese people have shown the greatest tolerance over the whole series of hostile actions of the British Government and the Hong Kong British authorities. However, the tolerance of the Chinese people cannot be limitless. Should the British Government and the Hong Kong British authorities continue to provoke the Chinese people, they must be prepared for all the possible consequences.

CHINESE COMMUNIST
POLICY TOWARD JAPAN

[*Note:* The following article from the official Chinese Communist organ, the *People's Daily,* provides a good example of the Chinese Communist viewpoint and policy toward Japan. Large sectors of the Japanese press have been highly resentful over the Peking line that the Japanese government does not represent the Japanese people, but Peking has been able to exploit the Japanese need for trade by playing off the individual needs and hopes of diverse groups in Japan against the government with which rests the responsibility for Japanese security. In October of 1958, leftist groups, with inspiration as well as pressure from Communist China, were pressing for a new united front in Japan for the purposes of expelling United States bases from Japan, Okinawa, and Taiwan; breaking the United States-Japanese alliance; recognition for Peking; and toppling of the Kishi government.]

"Observer" in the People's Daily, *September 16, 1958.*

A joint statement has been issued by Japanese Foreign Minister Aiichiro Fujiyama and U.S. Secretary of State John Foster Dulles following their talks held during Fujiyama's visit to the United States on September 11 and 12. Referring to the situation in the Taiwan Strait, the joint statement slanderously charged that "the use of force by Communist China created grave tension in the Far East and that interna-

147

tional communism remains the major threat to peace in the Far East." This again shows that the Japanese Kishi government's policy of subservience toward the United States and hostility toward China has not changed a single bit.

Japan's economic crisis is being deepened and perpetuated. The Japanese people are dissatisfied with the Kishi government's begging of alms from the United States to comply with the Japanese monopolists' economic expansion in Southeast Asia. They have demanded that the Kishi government change its policy of subservience to the United States and hostility toward China, coexist with China peacefully and adopt a sincere attitude toward the Asian countries. The Japanese people believe that this is the road to Japan's peaceful development and prosperity. Expression of this demand is growing.

The pressure of the people and public opinion in Japan forced Fujiyama to say in the Japanese Diet before his departure for the United States that the Japanese Government "does not recognize two Chinas" and that the "Taiwan problem is China's domestic problem." On Sept. 1 he told a House committee that "for historical and geographical reasons, there exist between Japan and China feelings which are not necessarily found in Sino-American relations" and that he "would endeavor to obtain better recognition of these feelings" from the United States. It is clear now that these words were only a smoke screen to fool the Japanese people and public opinion and were gestures of bargaining with the United States. True enough, within two weeks Fujiyama is again singing to the tune of Dulles and slandering China.

It is known that the present grave tension in the Taiwan Strait is entirely due to the arrogant intervention in China's internal affairs by the United States and its expansion of aggressive activities in the islands of China's inland sea, Quemoy and Matsu. U.S. military bases and troops in Japan and Okinawa have already been used to intensify this tension.

The punishment by the Chinese people of the Chiang Kai-shek clique elements, who have frequently engaged in harassments from the offshore islands, and the liberation by the Chinese people of their own territories at a time and by means which they consider suitable, is entirely their own affair. But for U.S. intervention, there would be no question of "Far Eastern tension." It is the United States and no one else that has deliberately created and maintained tension in the Far East. It is the Kishi government of Japan which has followed the United States, supplied it with military bases and tried to absolve it of the crime of aggression. Fujiyama's singing of the same tune as Dulles fully testifies to the fact that this paper's previous revelation and analysis of the latent imperialist nature of the Kishi government was absolutely correct and necessary.

Fujiyama's attitude toward the Taiwan Strait situation as shown in his joint statement with Dulles sharply contrasts with "the basic policy for breaking the deadlock between Japan and China" recently issued by the Japanese Socialist Party, as well as the statements and resolutions on the Taiwan question released by the Japanese Communist Party and various peace and democratic organizations in Japan. This clearly reflects the struggle between the two roads now being waged in Japan.

One is to follow the United States and, in accordance with U.S. intentions to conspire with the Chiang Kai-shek and Syngman Rhee cliques to form a Northeast Asian anti-Communist alliance, to permit the United States permanently to keep its military bases in Japan and to step up Japan's joining the U.S. atomic strategy system in an attempt to use the strength of the United States to revive the imperialist dream. This is the road of the Nobusuke Kishi government.

The other road is to get rid of U.S. control, to demand that the United States abolish its military bases and withdraw its troops in Japan, to demand the return of Okinawa, to demand that the Kishi government give up its hostile policy to China and its plot to create "two Chinas," cease obstructing the restoration of normal relations between China and Japan, coexist peacefully with China, and oppose U.S. interference in China's internal affairs, and U.S. aggravation of Far Eastern tension by means of military bases in Japan. This is the road that the broad masses of Japanese people want to follow. To the Japanese people, the former means war and calamity, while the latter promises peace and prosperity.

During his visit to the United States, Fujiyama showed that he sought a "higher degree of coordination" with the United States and to tie Japan further to the U.S. war chariot. On the Taiwan question he openly supported U.S. aggression. This again exposed his out-and-out hostile attitude to China. This is not only intolerable to the Chinese people but will arouse even greater opposition on the part of the Japanese people.

By following the United States in stepping up tension in the Far East, the Kishi government will gain nothing except to reap what it sows.

INDEX BY NAME

INDEX BY SUBJECT